VOLUME

4

REAL ESTATE CLOSING

Settlement Agent

ISBN-13: 978-1-933039-21-3

Library of Congress -in-Publication Data
January 2008

Real Estate Settlement
Closing Agent Basic Training

Printed in the United States of America

10 9 8 7 6 5 4 3 2 1

The enclosed material is designed for educational purposes only. Each State may have different certification and specific guidelines. Please refer to your State for additional and future information. The information contained herein is considered correct at the time of creation but laws and regulations are updated frequently and the reader assumes the responsibility for confirming current regulations and applicable data. The publisher and author make no warranty as to the success of the individuals using the training material contained herein. The publisher and author make no warranty as to any action taken by any individual completing this program. The reader is responsible for the appropriate use of the materials and information provided. This publication is designed to provide accurate and authoritative information concerning the subject matter. All material is sold with the understanding that neither the author nor the publisher guarantees the actions of any individual making use of the inclusions. Neither the author nor the publisher is rendering a legal opinion, accounting recommendation or other professional service. If legal advice or other expert assistance is desired, the services of a legal professional or other individual should be sought. The applicable federally released forms, disclosures and notices are generated from public domain. Copyright law does apply to all intellectual materials and all rights under said law are reserved by the copyright owner.

Coursework is available at special quantity discounts to use as premiums and sales promotions within corporate or private training programs. To obtain information or inquire about availability please write to Director, PO Box 1, Hollidaysburg, PA 16648.

NOTICE

REAL ESTATE CLOSING

Settlement Agent

Introduction	Title Closing	1
Chapter 1	Types of Meetings	4
Chapter 2	Party Obligations	8
Chapter 3	Meeting Overviews	12
Chapter 4	Opening Escrow	19
Chapter 5	Potential Delays	22
Chapter 6	The Sales Contract	24
Chapter 7	The Title Search	47
Chapter 8	Deeds	51
Chapter 9	How Title Is Held	69
Chapter 10	Loan Commitment and Security	74
Chapter 11	Verifications and Certifications	94
Chapter 12	Pro-Rata Calculations	117
Chapter 13	HUD 1 Settlement Statement	126
Chapter 14	Signing and Post Close	140
Chapter 15	RESPA	144
Appendix A	Expanded Course Guide	147
Appendix B	Glossary of Terms	149
Appendix C	Study Guide	153

Title Closing

Title closing is the time when a real estate transfer or purchase transaction is completed. Specific terminology may vary by region and other common terms used to describe this transaction include closing escrow or holding a settlement meeting. Regardless of terminology, the results of the closing are the same, a completed real estate transfer where all contractual items are fulfilled and both parties' obligations are legally settled. These transfers often require the services of a trained real estate settlement agent.

The purpose behind having a trained settlement agent oversee the closing process is to provide an impartial third party who will finalize all of the transaction details. This ensures that the transaction is closed in a fair manner and that all parties fulfill their contractual obligations. The title used to describe a settlement agent may also vary by region. Closing agent or escrow agent are commonly heard titles used in relationship to this position.

The form of the meeting will change by region and in relationship to the accepted understanding of the processes behind the different terms used to define the closings. The most common types of closing meeting terminology you will encounter include the round table settlement and the escrow. The differences between the actual processes incorporated into these two forms of closings and the accepted form and flow to each type of meeting is detailed for you in later chapters. To assist you in gaining the most effective training, you should confirm the types of closings typically held in your region. This will assist you as you complete your coursework and allow you to apply the training incorporated into the following chapters to the specific type of closing you will oversee.

During the closing process, there are common components that you will oversee regardless of specific naming, contractual contingencies or transaction variations.

- The buyer will make payment for the property.

  The payment could include funds from a variety of sources including gift funds, seller concessions, loan funding or any other source available to the borrower. As the settlement agent, you must confirm that the funds brought to the closing by the borrower equal the total entered on the settlement statement.

  Each type of funding that the buyer may obtain could contain specific contingencies or requirements as a part of the agreement to provide these funds. As the settlement agent, you must confirm that all of the contingencies and agreements are completed per the agreement in order to obtain the right to release the applicable funds.

- The seller delivers the deed to the property.

  The deed may be prepared by the company for which you work or come from another source such as the seller's attorney. As the settlement agent, you should confirm that the deed type, warranty inclusions and other entries are correct and match the transaction specifics from the other transaction documents exactly.

- All pertinent transaction documents are reviewed and signed.

  Transaction documents will vary depending on the needs of the parties involved in the transfer. It is the function of the settlement agent to review each document for accuracy and completeness, provide the documents to the parties for signature, give basic explanations of the documents purpose, and to witness the signing of the documents.

  It should be noted that as a settlement agent, you might explain the purpose of the documents; however, your function does not include offering legal advice to any party in the transaction. If any question pertaining to the transaction or applicable documents arise that requires an explanation, the buyer and the seller should be directed to the applicable affinity service provider for that clarification and explanation.

Example: The buyer's mortgage paperwork does not match the expectations of the buyer.

The buyer should contact their mortgage lender for an explanation as to why the inclusions of the paperwork do not match the disclosures or explanations previously provided.

You may explain the general purpose of the mortgage, note and loan documents but should direct the buyer to the lending representative for specific explanations of the transaction.

- All funds relating to pro-rata or negotiated exchanges are transferred.

  All expenses and credits pertaining to the transaction will be detailed on the HUD 1 or settlement statement. You will provide this statement to each party and briefly review the figures entered. The parties should take this review opportunity to confirm that the transaction specifics match the expectations set for them during the negotiation process.

- All bills incurred in relationship to the property or the transaction are paid

  Often, closing expenses are paid during the negotiation period leading to the closing; however, some expenses may remain outstanding at the time of the settlement meeting. These expenses should be entered on the HUD 1 and it is the function of the settlement agent to ensure that all matters are confirmed with the parties. The entries should match the negotiation of who is responsible for each expense relating to the transaction or property.

  Common expenses handled at the closing include utility payments incurred at the property, appraisal costs relating to the transaction and the closing fee paid to your company for your services.

- Other functions as deemed appropriate to the transaction may occur at the settlement meeting such as the assignment of lease agreement documents, the completion of mortgage documents or the transfer of property insurance.

The list includes many of the most common components of the settlement meeting; however, it is important to remember that it is not all-inclusive. As each transaction is different; therefore, the functions of the settlement agent at the closing will be different each time a transaction is closed. It is the job of the settlement agent to confirm that all details specific to the transaction, contingencies written into the sales contract and requirements for close as detailed within the closing instructions are met by the parties involved in the transaction. The following chapters will assist you in gaining a better understanding of the tasks you may perform in relationship to the closing. The chapters also outline the actions and tasks that may occur outside of your realm but have an impact on your closing.

CHAPTER

1

TYPES OF MEETINGS

Title Closing refers to the completion of the real estate transaction. The closing is the time set aside for the buyer to pay for the property, the seller to deliver the deed to the property and for all details negotiated between the parties to be finalized. The day that these items occur is termed the closing date, settlement or escrow. In some regions, the closing is completed at a meeting where all parties to the transaction and their agents come together at the same place and time. In other regions, an escrow agent conducts the closing. This agent completes all necessary tasks based upon a series of instructions and then sends the finalized documents and funds to each party of the transaction.

ROUND TABLE OR ESCROW

The exact format and processes of the settlement you oversee will vary depending on the region of the country in which you are conducting your business.

In some regions, the closing process will be termed a roundtable settlement. At a roundtable closing, all parties pertinent to the transaction will be present at the settlement meeting to complete all of the negotiated items required for the legal transfer of the subject property.

REAL ESTATE CLOSING - SETTLEMENT AGENT

As the name implies, a round table closing dictates that all parties pertinent to the transaction will sit down simultaneously to complete their legal requirements. The buyer and seller, as well as any chosen representatives, will be present. The buyer and the seller are the primary parties who must attend the closing meeting; however, other individuals relating to the transaction or chosen by either the buyer or the seller might attend.

- A real estate agent who represents the buyer, the seller or both may attend the closing meeting.

- Either party may retain the services of an attorney to protect their interests in the transaction. If an attorney has been retained, they may be present at the closing.

- The buyer will often have a home mortgage loan relating to the transaction and a representative from the lending company may be present.

These are the most common outside parties who may attend the settlement meeting. Each of these individuals has an interest in the transaction and may wish to review the closing documents you provide for signature at the meeting. It is important that you provide these individuals with the opportunity to review the closing documents prior to the signing. This review opportunity will enable the applicable individual to confirm the inclusions of the transaction are as expected, are as negotiated and contain the specifics negotiated on previous agreements. This review should occur before any signatures are affixed to any document. This ability to review the documents is subject to the approval of the buyer and seller.

Other individuals as deemed appropriate and desirable by either party may attend the closing though these are the most common parties.

During the closing, you will provide the documents that must be signed to the applicable parties in order to finalize the transaction. It is a critical portion of your function at the meeting to confirm that all necessary signatures are obtained and to witness these signatures.

All transactions meant to convey the legal ownership of a piece of real property would contain specific actions. The two most common items that will pertain to the closings you will oversee are that the seller will deliver the deed to the buyer and the buyer will deliver the purchase funds, if any, to the seller.

- The delivery of funds by the buyer may be completed using cash, a mortgage note signed by the buyer or other means of payment as negotiated during the sales contract period. Each method of delivery of funds may require other documents, which you must provide for signature.

    Example: When a mortgage loan is secured for the transaction, additional documents might become part of the closing. These could include items such as a promissory note, a finalized mortgage application, and additional documents specific to the lender funding the loan.

When you are providing settlement services for a transaction that contains a mortgage, the lender will often provide a set of closing instructions specific to their needs in the transaction.

These instructions outline the requirements, documents for signature, and transaction specifics that must occur in order for the lender to transfer purchase funds to the closing company. The transaction cannot be considered finalized until these funds are received and dispersed according to the contracts of the transaction so complying with the inclusions of the lender instructions is a critical function.

You must review the closing instructions and confirm that each task set forth is completed per the requirements of the lender.

- During the closing, all matters negotiated in the sales agreement will be reviewed and confirmation that all stipulations have been met will be made by both the buyer and the seller.

The sales agreement will typically contain all of the details negotiated between the parties that must be completed prior to the transfer of the property. You should review the sales agreement, any addendums to the agreement and the specific contingencies negotiated within the agreement to confirm that all tasks set forth have been completed by the parties prior to beginning the settlement meeting.

- The individuals legally required to sign each document will attend the settlement and affix their signature to all of the necessary documents.

If the buyer or seller is unable to attend the closing or another individual expected to attend is unable to be present, a representative will be appointed. This representative will hold power of attorney or another legal authorization that enables them to act on behalf of the missing party.

As the settlement agent, you must confirm the power of these individuals to act on behalf of the missing party and witness the signatures of this individual in place of the applicable party.

Each individual who attends the closing will have specific responsibilities in relationship to the legal finalization of the transaction. These specifics will vary by transaction and it is the duty of the settlement agent to confirm that all tasks set forth in the sales agreement; addendums to the agreement, mortgage documents and other negotiation instruments specific to the transaction are completed according to the entries or instructions on each document.

REAL ESTATE CLOSING - SETTLEMENT AGENT

A transaction cannot be considered finalized until every task has been completed or a waiver nullifying the need for a specifically negotiated item has been received from the applicable parties.

You should review all documents that contain closing instructions or transaction negotiations prior to the meeting to confirm that you understand all of the items that must be completed. You should then generate a task list if one has not been provided. This task list should detail every act, signature and applicable confirmation that must occur to reach the final legal transfer of the property. Before releasing any individual from the settlement meeting, you must review your task list and confirm that they have competed all of their obligations in the transaction. This confirmation of task completion will assist you in conducting smooth settlement meetings and assist you in gaining a reputation as a settlement agent who provides flawless closings.

CHAPTER 2

PARTY OBLIGATIONS

To ensure the closing process proceeds smoothly, all parties attending the meeting are responsible for bringing certain items or documents. The settlement agent is reasonable for contacting each party and confirming that they understand the items they are to bring with them to the closing.

SELLER'S RESPONSIBILITY

The seller or the seller's attorney must bring or arrange to have certain documents at the closing table. At times, the settlement agent or title company will accept responsibility for providing these documents. The required items will be detailed on the negotiation documents pertinent to the transaction. The specifics of these items will vary by the transaction. The most common items may include

- the executable deed including any covenants and warranties agreed upon by the parties

- the most recent property tax bill for the property being transferred

- an insurance policy showing current coverage on the property if such a requirement has been negotiated in the sales agreement

- the termite or other inspection as negotiated within the sales agreement

- deeds or documents showing the removal of any liens or encumbrances discovered during the title search or required by the negotiated sales agreement or lender commitment

- a title commitment and insurance policy

- a survey or survey affidavit as required

- an offset statement or statement by an owner or lien holder as to the exact balance due on a lien held against the property

- keys to the property

- if the property is an income producing property, any documents securing or confirming this income will also be required. These might include leases, rent schedules, P&L Statements and proof that notification of the pending transfer has been delivered to the individuals making said income payments

While these are the most common items that the seller will be responsible for in relationship to the closing, any other item pertinent to the transaction may become part of your closing package. Each transaction is different due to the negotiations of the parties involved so you must be prepared to assess and handle any situation that may arise.

BUYERS RESPONSIBILITY

The buyer is responsible for having funds available for the purchase price negotiated for the property, settlement costs and any matters that the buyer has agreed to pay on or before settlement.

In many cases, the buyer will obtain a loan to cover many of the costs of the purchase and settlement. The buyer must bring a loan commitment to the settlement meeting. The Mortgage Lender will often work directly with the settlement company and if it does, it will provide the loan commitment and applicable closing instructions directly to your offices.

All conditions of this loan commitment must be met prior to the final closing of the new loan and therefore the closing of the property. At times, the lender will work directly with the closing company and provide all documents and instructions pertinent to the transaction directly to your company. You will be responsible for confirming the signature on all documents requested by the lender and for confirming the completion of the acts detailed on the closing instructions.

- The lender will provide a check or wire transfer to the settlement company in the amount of the agreed upon loan.

- The lender will provide specific documents for the buyer to sign at the settlement meeting. These could include a mortgage, note, riders, addendums and any other document they deem necessary to solidify the repayment requirement of the funds provided for the transaction.

If the lender chooses not to attend the closing, the applicable funds, documents and specific instructions will be provided to the buyer or to the settlement company in charge of the closing.

The buyer will be required to provide in the form of a certified check or money order, any additional funds required beyond the loan provided.

The buyer will typically be required to provide a form of identification to prove their identity to the individual conducting the settlement meeting.

ESCROW AGENT

The escrow agent will begin the process of opening escrow by confirming four essential elements of the transaction.

1. Determine if a valid contract exists, that illustrates the negotiations of the transaction.

2. Confirm that all parties to the transactions are legally authorized to conduct legal actions through competency, resident status and legal age verification.

3. Verify that each party is being fairly compensated for the exchange being made through the transaction.

4. Determine that a legal parcel or property is being transferred between the parties.

Upon confirmation that the four essential elements that create a legal contract exist, the escrow agent will order the escrow process to begin. The escrow agent will use the real estate purchase agreement as a guide to the tasks that must be completed in order for the transaction to close.

The following chapters will assist you in gaining the knowledge you require to complete the steps necessary for the smooth closing of a transaction.

TIMETABLE	
Week 1	Receive Escrow Order Review Sales Contract
Week 1 – 2	Order Preliminary Title Report Open Escrow Account Order Pest Inspections Comply with Sale Agreement Terms / Orders
Week 3	Receive Lender Instructions Review Preliminary Title Report Review Inspections Order Pay Off Summary or Defect Cure Actions Indicated by the Title Report
Week 3-4	Prepare Escrow Instructions Complete Pro-Rata Calculations Generate Settlement Statement Prepare Loan Documents

Week 4	Hold Settlement Meeting
	Sign Documents
	Close Escrow
	Record Documents
	Release Funds
	Pay off all matters

Figure 2:1 Sample Closing Process Timetable

CHAPTER

3

MEETING OVERVIEW

Now that you understand the parties who will attend the meeting and the components that will be common to a settlement meeting, you should review the flow of a settlement meeting, as it will most often occur. It is important that you understand that closings will vary by the negotiations of the parties and the flow provided is an example of the best practices only. Specific transactions that you attend may vary from the best practice flow described.

ROUND TABLE MEETING

- All parties to the transaction will arrive at the meeting.

  In some cases, an individual may have arranged to sign all of the required documents and provide any necessary items to the settlement agent prior to the date of the closing. If this is the case, the applicable individual may not attend the actual settlement.

  A representative may have been appointed by one of the parties to act on their behalf at the settlement meeting. This representative will hold a power of attorney that authorizes them to complete all legal matters required of the party to finalize the transaction. In this event, the representative will attend.

- The settlement agent will record the legal names of all parties present at the meeting and note these parties as either signors or witnesses to the transaction.

  Most states require that the settlement agent obtain a copy of a legal form of identification for each party who will be signing documents.

- The settlement statement, which may also be termed a closing statement or HUD 1, is provided to the buyer and the seller for inspection.

  The settlement statement summarizes all financial aspects of the transaction.

  You should review the settlement statement and compare it to the negotiation instruments prior to the settlement meeting. This review will enable you to address any variations prior to the meeting and locate mistakes before all parties are present at the table.

- The seller will execute the deed and provide it to the buyer.

- The buyer and/or lender provide a check to the seller in the negotiated amount.

  The check provided to the seller will typically be in the amount listed as the final figure to the seller on the HUD 1.

  The settlement agent will often retain a portion of the funds present at the closing table to pay service providers and complete other financial transactions as deemed necessary and as disclosed on the settlement statement.

  Some closings are termed dry closings. At a dry closing, the funds from a lender will not be present at the time of the closing. These funds will be transferred to the settlement agent and become available for disbursement upon confirmation by the lender that all loan conditions have been satisfied.

  > At this type of closing, the seller will receive their final check after the closing has been finalized.

  > All parties will complete the required documents and entrust them to the individual in charge of the closing.

  > No money is disbursed and the deed is not delivered until the missing paperwork or funds arrive.

  > When the missing documents or funds arrive, the settlement agent completes the transaction and delivers the funds or documents by mail or messenger to the applicable parties.

- The buyer will sign any mortgage, note or other document provided by the lender in return for the obtainment of the funds.

  The required documents and actions that must be completed will be detailed on the closing instructions provided by the mortgage lender.

  You should review these instructions prior to the settlement meeting to confirm that all necessary documents are present and that all inclusions on the instructions can be satisfied during the meeting.

- Following closing the new deed, mortgage and note will be recorded. If additional recordable documents were required to complete the transaction, these will also be recorded.

ESCROW

In some areas of the country, the title closing is conducted by an escrow agent who is a neutral third party selected by both the buyer and the seller. The term escrow agent is functionally used to refer to the settlement agent; however, the specifics of the meeting will vary somewhat from a round table settlement. The escrow agent will complete all essentials of the transaction without the requirement of actually holding a round table meeting. The process followed will be similar in that all pertinent actions negotiated and documents required will be completed, however the timeline and actual form of the closing will be different from the round table meeting.

- The sales agreement will be negotiated between the buyer and the seller.

- An escrow agent will be chosen by the buyer and seller.

  The escrow agent will be a neutral third party entrusted with the responsibility of handling all details of the transaction.

  The escrow agent may be

  - a bank or savings institution

  - another lending agency

  - an independent escrow company

  - an attorney

  - an escrow department of a title insurance company

> ➢ a real estate broker providing the real estate broker is not earning a sales commission through the completion of the transaction

> ➢ another individual licensed and bonded to complete this type of service

- The buyer or real estate agent representing the buyer will provide the escrow agent with the earnest money deposit and a copy of the negotiated sales contract.

  The escrow agent will deposit the earnest money deposit into a special bank account.

- The escrow agent will prepare a set of escrow instructions based upon the signed sales contract.

  These instructions detail, in writing, every action that each party must complete before the transaction is finalized.

- The escrow agent will typically order a title search on the property being transferred. At times, the burden of fulfilling this title search requirement may be placed upon either the buyer or the seller instead of the escrow agent or company.

  When the title search is complete, either the search details or insurance commitment will be forwarded to the buyer or attorney representing the buyer for review and approval.

- If an existing loan is being repaid as part of the transaction, the escrow agent will contact the lender to whom the funds are due to obtain a statement of the exact funds required to complete the pay off.

  The escrow agent will also request a mortgage release from the lender. This will be recorded at the county courthouse as part of the transaction.

- If an existing loan is to be assumed by the buyer as part of the transaction, the escrow agent will obtain the current loan balance and any documents required by the buyer or the seller to complete the loan assumption.

- The seller will provide the deed to the escrow agent.

  This deed will be fully executed prior to delivery. Once delivered, if the seller becomes incapacitated or incapable of completing the transaction, all matters will proceed without the seller's presence.

- The seller will provide property insurance, tax papers and proof of tax payment status to the escrow agent.

- The escrow agent will prorate all tax, insurance or other payments required and include these figures on the settlement or closing statement.

- The seller will provide copies of any leases, contracts or other documents pertaining to income produced by the property being transferred to the escrow agent.

  The escrow agent will prorate all income matters as negotiated by the sales agreement and include these figures on the settlement or closing statement.

- Any matters negotiated in the sales agreement or required by the lender will be remitted to the escrow agent for confirmation of completion.

- The closing agent will confirm all matters as negotiated have been satisfied and the final funds request will be sent to the buyer or lender for the buyer.

- Any matters required by the lender as part of the loan commitment to provide funds will be forwarded to the escrow agent. The escrow agent will typically ensure all matters included in the loan commitment are remitted to the lender and the conditions necessary for funding are satisfied.

- The required funds will be remitted to the escrow agent and deposited into a special trust account to be held for release on the date of closing.

- Any final documents requiring the signature of any party will be signed and notarized.

- The escrow agent will order a final check on title the day before closing to confirm that no changes to the condition of title have occurred since the date of the full exam.

- The deed, mortgage, mortgage release and other documents pertaining to the transaction will be recorded.

- Upon confirmation of recording, the escrow agent will provide a check to any party to whom funds are due as part of the transaction.

- The escrow agent will provide final copies of any documents relating to the transaction.

At this point, the transaction is considered closed and the property transferred to the new owner. The form of the closing requirements is the same as that which completes a round table settlement, however the methodology used to complete the transaction is different. It is important that you confirm the type of meeting common in your State prior to moving forward with your training.

This confirmation will enable you to apply the information contained in the following chapters specifically to the type of transaction you will oversee.

CHAPTER

4

OPENING ESCROW

Many tasks will occur prior to the meeting. Each of these tasks creates a portion of the package that will be finalized by you, the settlement agent, at the closing. The following chapters will help you to gain a better understanding of those tasks that will be completed prior to you beginning your actual settlement functions. Learning each of the actions that occur to lead to closing and how each of those items will relate to the actions you must complete during the actual closing meeting will assist you in becoming a knowledgeable settlement agent, well versed in all facets of settlement and capable of answering the questions that might arise at the settlement table.

The closing company for which you work will receive an order to open escrow or begin the process. The first task upon receipt of a new order is to review the information included in the order and confirm that all of the data that will be needed to proceed is included within the ordering documents. If items are missing from the order or the information included is incomplete, individuals involved in the transaction will need to be contacted to confirm the ordering information. Upon receipt, you should look for the following basic information.

- Date of the Order

- Property address

- The names and addresses of all owners who hold interest in the property

- The full name and address of the buyer(s) of the property

- The sales price agreed upon for the purchase of the property

- The amount (if any) of the earnest money paid

- The allocation of the earnest money

- Any contingencies that effect the earnest money deposit

- The amount, if any, of additional funds placed in escrow or other locations to be credited toward the transaction.

- The financial specifics including any seller finance, seller concessions, lender funds and any conditions relating to these financial matters

- The name of the real estate agent, if any, handling the transaction as well as the commission payment that the real estate agent will receive in the transaction

- Commissions or fees to be paid to other affinity service providers

- Any mortgages or other financial matters that must be cleared prior to the transfer of the property

- Property description and sale inclusions or exclusions

- Any inspections or reports noted within the contracts that must be satisfactorily received prior to the finalization of the transaction

- Individual or parties to whom the initial title report, payoffs and other matters will be sent.

   This could be the buyer, the seller, the real estate agent, the lender or another party pertinent to your transaction

- The exact names of the individuals who will be taking title to the property

- The expected close date and specific dates for action within the process

REAL ESTATE CLOSING - SETTLEMENT AGENT
ESCROW PROPERTY:

Date: _____ Ordering Individual: _____

Subject Property: _____

Owner: _____ Co-Owner: _____

Address: _____

Telephone Number: _____ Alternate Number: _____

Buyer: _____ Co-Buyer: _____

Current Address: _____

Telephone Number: _____ Alternate Number: _____

TRANSACTION DETAILS

Sales Price: $_____ Earnest Money Paid: _____

Total Down Payment (Including Deposit: $_____

Other Finance Specifics: _____

_____

Seller Agent Commission: $_____ ___% Paid to: _____

Buyer Agent Commission: $_____ ___% Paid to: _____

1st Mortgage Lender: _____ Amount: _____

Terms: _____

Other liens to be paid: _____ Amount: _____

Terms: _____

Inspections and Reports: _____

_____

Closing Date: _____ Closing Costs: _____

Special Closing Notes: _____

_____

Names to appear on title: _____

_____

Other Notes: _____

CHAPTER

5

POTENTIAL DELAYS

The expected closing date for a real estate transaction will typically be included on the negotiated sales contract. This expected close date is agreed upon between the buyer and the seller at the time the sales contact is written. This date sets the timeline for all functions that must occur to close the loan.

T he determination of when the closing date is set will depend on a variety of factors.

The date the buyer wishes to take possession will be considered.

The date the seller wishes to relinquish possession of the property and obtain the purchase funds will play a role.

Often the determining factor with the highest impact will be the timeline that the affinity service providers feel they require to complete the services necessary to close the transaction. The items that the affinity service providers will consider before agreeing to an expected close date include:

- the completion of the loan application and documentation process to obtain the required purchase money

- the completion of a title search on the subject property

- the issuance of a title insurance policy

- the completion of an appraisal

- the completion of a termite or other inspection report as desired by the buyer, seller or mortgage lender

- the completion of any other matter negotiated on the contract and required to be completed prior to the date of closing

In a typical real estate transaction, it may take between 15 and 60 days to complete all of the required items, searches, inspections, loan stipulations and other matters as negotiated within the sales contract. An average time for closing of a home loan is 30 days from the date that the sales contract is finalized between the buyer and the seller. The functions of the settlement agent will often be the last items requiring completion in the transaction.

Delays may sometimes occur that cause a requirement to extend the expected closing date beyond that negotiated on the sales contract. When this occurs and it becomes apparent that the agreed upon close date will note be met, an addendum to the sales agreement must be created that extends the closing date agreement. This addendum must be signed by both parties to be considered valid. Typically, if the delay is for a reasonable period and cause, the extension will be granted. Some contracts allow for the real estate broker representing either party to extend the contract. If the delay will be lengthy, create undue hardship for either party or is objectionable to either party, a release will be signed by both the buyer and the seller relieving all parties from their obligations under the contract. If this release occurs, then the transaction is cancelled and is legally considered to have never happened. If this occurs and there are service bills outstanding, it is important that you have the billings paid by the party who is deemed responsible for the cancellation or is detailed as the responsible party within the contracts.

If the transaction is to continue toward the expected close date, it is important that the title or escrow company complete any tasks set forth on their task list in a timely manner. This helps to ensure that they are not the cause for a delay in the closing process. As a settlement agent, you may work independent of a title company or Escrow Company and therefore the flow of the transaction might be out of your control, however it is important to understand the actions that must occur and the timeline that must be met in order to reach a close and for your services to be required.

CHAPTER

6

THE SALES CONTRACT

A sales agreement that is correctly prepared and endorsed is a binding contract that holds each applicable party responsible for the terms negotiated within the contract. Once the sales agreement is written and signed, all parties are obligated to complete the transaction providing the terms of the contract can be legally met. Part of the function of the escrow agent it to facilitate the ability of each party to meet the obligations and agreements dictated within the sales contract.

T he sales agreement will dictate the handling of many matters with regard to both the pre-close activities and the actual closing of the real estate being transferred. It is critical that escrow or settlement agent become familiar with all entries on a real estate sales contract and the proper action dictated by each item included within the contract.

A sales agreement may take many forms and include all of the entries on the example included for your review, additional entries created by the parties involved in the transaction or just some of the entries. If a sales agreement is privately created between the buyer and the seller, some information essential to the settlement agent may not be included. It is up to the agent to confirm that all required details are included in the sales contract or to gain the necessary information from the buyer and the seller prior to proceeding with the settlement documents.

REAL ESTATE CLOSING - SETTLEMENT AGENT

The following pages include explanations for each section of the standard real estate sales contract that are most critical to the escrow and settlement process. Additional sections and clauses are included for your review. You should gain a basic familiarity with all areas of a standard residential sales agreement and focus more intensely on those sections detailed in the following pages that apply directly to the escrow processes or settlement actions.

It is important to remember that a sales agreement may take many forms and that addenda can be created to the sales agreement. Addenda will typically address items of specific importance to the parties involved and will often create additional requirements or negotiations and transaction handling that differs from a common transaction. Any alteration to the sales agreement should be scrutinized to ensure that the settlement agent completes each action required of the transaction according to the expectations of the involved parties.

KENNEY

STANDARD AGREEMENT FOR THE SALE OF REAL ESTATE

SELLERS BUISNES RELATIONSHIP WITH LICENSED BROKER
Broker (company) _____ Phone _____
Address _____ Fax _____
Licensee(s) _____ Designated Agent __ Yes __ No
BROKER IS THE AGNET FOR THE SELLER   OR (if checked below):
Broker is NOT the Agent for the seller and is a/an: __ AGENT FOR BUYER __ Transaction Licensee

BUYERS BUISNES RELATIONSHIP WITH LICENSED BROKER
Broker (company) _____ Phone _____
Address _____ Fax _____
Licensee(s) _____ Designated Agent __ Yes __ No
BROKER IS THE AGNET FOR THE BUYER   OR (if checked below):
Broker is NOT the Agent for the seller and is a/an: __ AGENT FOR SELLER __ Transaction Licensee

When the same Broker is Agent for Buyer, Broker is a Dual Agent. All of Broker's licensees are also Dual Agents UNLESS there is a separate Designated Agents for Buyer and Seller. If the same Licensee is designated for Seller and Buyer, the Licensee is a Dual Agent.

1. *This Agreement*, dated _____ is between SELLER(S): _____, called Seller, and
BUYER(S): _____ , called Buyer.

2. PROPERTY Seller herby agrees to sell and convey to Buyer, who hereby agrees to purchase:
ALL THAT CERTAIN lot or piece of ground with buildings and improvements thereon erected, if any, known as:
_____
_____
In the _____ of _____ County of _____ in the State of
_____. Identification (e.g., Tax ID#, Parcel #; Lot, Block; Deed Book, Page,
Recording Date): _____

3. TERMS
(A) Purchase Price _____
_____ U.S. Dollars
which will be paid to the Seller by the Buyer as follows:
   1. Cash or check at the signing of this Agreement_____ $ _____
   2. Cash or check within _____ days of the execution of this agreement_____ $ _____
   3. _____ _____ $ _____
   4. Cash or cashiers check at the time of settlement_____ $ _____
                     TOTAL $ _____

(B) Deposits paid by Buyer within _____ DAYS of settlement will be by cash or cashiers check. Deposits, regardless of the form of payment and the person designated as payee, will be paid in U.S. Dollars to Broker for Seller (unless otherwise stated here) _____
_____ who will retain deposits in an escrow account until consummation or termination of this Agreement in conformity with all applicable laws and regulations. Any check tendered as deposit monies may be held uncashed pending the acceptance of this agreement.

(C) Seller's written approval to be on or before _____

(D) Settlement to be on _____ or before if Buyer and Seller agree

(E) Settlement will occur in the county where the Property is located or in an adjacent county, during normal business hours, unless Buyer and Seller agree otherwise.

(F) Conveyance from Seller will be by fee simple deed of Special Warranty unless otherwise stated here _____
_____

(G) Payment of transfer taxes will be divided equally between Buyer and Seller unless otherwise stated here _____
_____

(H) At the time of settlement, the following will be adjusted pro-rata on a daily basis between Buyer and Seller, reimbursing where applicable current taxes (see Information regarding Real Estate Taxes), rents, interest on mortgage assumptions, condominium fees, and home owners association fees, water and or sewer fees together with any other lienable municipal services.

Figure 6:1 Sample Sales Contract Page 1

1. *This Agreement*, dated _____ is between SELLER(S):
    _____, called Seller, and
    BUYER(S): _____, called Buyer.

Figure 6:2 Sample Sales Contract Extraction

The full names of the buyers and the sellers of the transaction should be included on these lines of the sales agreement.

> The format of the name, including middle initial and exact spelling should match all of the other documents and instructions included within the package.

> If the form of the names vary from the other documents you have received, you should confirm how the names should appear on all final documents.

If any individual is named on the sales agreement but is not included within the deed and other transfer documents, you must confirm the inclusions.

All documents pertinent to the transaction should match in all ways. If there is a discrepancy, you must request correction of the document that contains the error.

2. PROPERTY Seller herby agrees to sell and convey to Buyer, who hereby agrees to purchase:
    ALL THAT CERTAIN lot or piece of ground with buildings and improvements thereon erected, if any, known as:
    _____
    _____
    In the _____ of _____ County of _____ in the State of
    _____. Identification (e.g., Tax ID#, Parcel #; Lot, Block; Deed Book, Page,
    Recording Date):

Figure 6:3 Sample Sales Contract Extraction

The property information should be included on the sales contract.

The description of the property including physical address, city name, county name and deed information should match all of the other documents in the transaction. If there is a discrepancy, you must request correction of the document that contains the error.

The individual overseeing the file and preparing the documents for closing will use the information entered on these forms to complete the title search and to generate the signature pages that will close the transaction.

---

3. TERMS
   (A) Purchase Price _____
   _____ U.S. Dollars
   which will be paid to the Seller by the Buyer as follows:
     1. Cash or check at the signing of this Agreement_____ $ _____
     2. Cash or check within ____ days of the execution of this agreement_____ $ _____
     3. _____ $ _____
     4. Cash or cashiers check at the time of settlement_____ $ _____
                       TOTAL $ _____

Figure 6:4 Sample Sales Contract Extraction

The financial details that occurred in an effort to finalize an agreement for the sale will often be included on the sales agreement.

Purchase Price	The purchase entry details the final agreed upon for the transaction.
	This figure will act as the basis for all other transaction calculations during the process.
Cash or check at Signing	This figure will be termed the earnest money deposit on your worksheet.
	It is important for the settlement agent to review the contingencies relating this deposit and determine exactly what will happen if the transaction is canceled. A deposit contingency will often outline the terms under which a buyer will be able to regain their earnest money deposit as well as those terms that shall result in a forfeiture of this deposit.
	The most common deposit item you will handle will be the method of applying the deposit to the transaction. The settlement statement should indicate the disposition and application of the deposit and it is a function of the settlement agent to confirm that the deposit is shown.
	If these details are not included, you must gain the necessary agreement information in order to have the funds applied correctly as the transaction progresses.
Additional Funds	At times, the buyer and seller may negotiate a transaction in which the buyer pays more than one deposit. If this is the case, the details of these additional payments should be outlined within the contract and the application of the funds should be detailed.

Signing Funds   The amount of money that remains due to the seller after the application of all deposit money will be detailed on the sales agreement. You should review these numbers to confirm that all funds listed add up to the sales price detailed on the contract. If there is a discrepancy, you should contact the Real Estate Agent if one is being used, or the buyer and seller to have the discrepancy corrected prior to proceeding.

Please note that these figures only pertain to the actual sales price money for the property. Details pertaining to a mortgage loan, closing costs, and other financial matters will usually not appear within this section of the sales agreement. You should confirm all applicable costs and financial arrangements to make certain you have an understanding of the full transaction details with regard to money.

(B) Deposits paid by Buyer within _____ DAYS of settlement will be by cash or cashiers check. Deposits, regardless of the form of payment and the person designated as payee, will be paid in U.S. Dollars to Broker for Seller (unless otherwise stated here) _____
_____ who will retain deposits in an escrow account until consummation or termination of this Agreement in conformity with all applicable laws and regulations. Any check tendered as deposit monies may be held uncashed pending the acceptance of this agreement.

Figure 6:5 Sample Sales Contract Extraction

The method of payment, term for payment and handling of the deposit money, both before and after the offer is accepted will be detailed here.

The contingencies pertaining to the application and / or return of the earnest money deposit will be included in a later chapter.

(C) Seller's written approval to be on or before _____
    (D) Settlement to be on _____ or before if Buyer and Seller agree
    (E) Settlement will occur in the county where the Property is located or in an adjacent county, during normal business hours, unless Buyer and Seller agree otherwise.

Figure 6:6 Sample Sales Contract Extraction

The dates pertinent to the transaction will be included within this section.

The most important date from the perspective of the settlement agent will be

"Settlement to be on _____ or before if buyer or seller agree."

The date entered on this line is the date that you will use to manage the flow of the transaction. All applicable actions and document should be completed on or before this date so that the transaction can close in compliance with the agreement. If all if the required items cannot be completed by this date, an extension agreement will need to be made between the buyer and the seller.

F) Conveyance from Seller will be by fee simple deed of Special Warranty unless otherwise stated here _____

Figure 6:7 Sample Sales Contract Extraction

The specific type of deed that the seller agrees to provide and the buyer agrees to accept will be detailed within the sales agreement. The chapter pertaining to deeds will provide you with clarification regarding how deed type variations effect the real estate transaction.

Regardless of whether your company or another completes the actual deed of conveyance, you should confirm that the type of deed and warranties contained within the deed match the entries on the sales agreement.

(G) Payment of transfer taxes will be divided equally between Buyer and Seller unless otherwise stated here _____
_____

(H) At the time of settlement, the following will be adjusted pro-rata on a daily basis between Buyer and Seller, reimbursing where applicable current taxes (see Information regarding Real Estate Taxes), rents, interest on mortgage assumptions, condominium fees, and home owners association fees, water and or sewer fees together with any other lienable municipal services.

Figure 6:8 Sample Sales Contract Extraction

The payment of transfer taxes and pro-rata calculations pertaining to other costs of the transaction will be detailed within the sales agreement.

You should note

- The division of transaction expenses outlined within the sales contract

- The date set for the pro-rata of fixed expense

The individual responsible for the preparation of the HUD 1 will calculate and verify the payments incorporated into this clause. These costs and pro-rata should be included in the Settlement Statement and you should confirm the inclusions prior to beginning the settlement meeting.

Additional details pertaining to pro-rata calculations are included in a later chapter.

REAL ESTATE CLOSING - SETTLEMENT AGENT

4. **FIXTURES & PERSONAL PROPERTY**
   (A) INCLUDED in this sale are all existing items, permanently installed in the Property, free of liens, including plumbing, heating, lighting fixtures (including chandeliers and ceiling fans); water treatment systems; pool and spa equipment; garage door openers and transmitters; television antennas; unspotted shrubbery, plantings and trees; any remaining heating and cooking fuels stored on the Property at the time of settlement; sump pumps; storage sheds; mailboxes; wall to wall carpeting; existing window screens, storm windows and screen storm doors, window covering hardware, shades and blinds; awnings; built-in air conditioners, built in appliances; and the range unless otherwise stated. Also included: _____
   (B) LEASED items (not owned by Seller): _____
   (C) EXCLUDED fixtures and items: _____

5. **DATES / TIME IS OF THE ESSENCE**
   (A) The settlement date and all other dates and times referred to for the performance of the obligations of this Agreement are of the essence and are binding.
   (B) For purposes of this Agreement, the number of days will be counted from the date of execution, excluding the day this Agreement was executed and including the last day of the time period. The Execution Date of this Agreement is the date when Buyer and Seller have indicated full acceptance of this Agreement by signing and/or initialing it. All changes to this Agreement should be initialed and dated.
   (C) The settlement date is not extended by any other provision of this Agreement and may only be extended by mutual written Agreement of the parties.
   (D) Certain time periods are pre-printed in this Agreement as a convenience to the Buyer and Seller. All pre-printed time periods are negotiable and may be changed by striking out the pre-printed text and inserting a different time period acceptable to all parties.

6. **MORTGAGE CONTINGENCY**
   ___ WAIVED This sales is NOT contingent on mortgage financing, although Buyer may still obtain mortgage financing.
   ___ ELECTED
   (A) The sale is contingent on Buyer obtaining mortgage financing as follows:

First Mortgage on the Property	Second Mortgage on the Property
Loan Amount $_____	Loan Amount $_____
Minimum Term _____ years	Minimum Term _____ years
Type of Mortgage _____	Type of Mortgage _____
Mortgage Lender _____	Mortgage Lender _____
_____	_____
Interest Rate _____% however, Buyer agrees to accept the interest rate as may be committed by the mortgage lender, not to exceed a maximum interest rate of _____%. Discount points, loan origination, loan placement, and other fees charged by the lender as a percentage of the mortgage loan (excluding any mortgage insurance premiums or VA funding fee) not to exceed _____% (1% if not specified)	Interest Rate _____% however, Buyer agrees to accept the interest rate as may be committed by the mortgage lender, not to exceed a maximum interest rate of _____%. Discount points, loan origination, loan placement, and other fees charged by the lender as a percentage of the mortgage loan (excluding any mortgage insurance premiums or VA funding fee) not to exceed _____% (1% if not specified)

The interest rate(s) and fee(s) provisions in paragraph 6(A) are satisfied if the mortgage lender(s) gives Buyer the right to guarantee the interest rate(s) and fee(s) at or before the maximum levels stated. Buyer gives Seller the right at Seller's sole option and as permitted by law and the mortgage lender(s) to contribute financially, without promise of reimbursement to the buyer and or the mortgage lender(s) to make the above mortgage terms available to the Buyer.
   (B) Within _____ days (10 if not specified) from the Execution Date of this Agreement, Buyer will make a completed, written mortgage application for the mortgage terms stated above to the mortgage lender(s) defined in paragraph 6(A), if any, otherwise to a responsible mortgage lender(s) of Buyer's choice. Broker for Buyer, if any, otherwise Broker for Seller, is authorized to communicate with the mortgage lender(s) to assist in the mortgage loan process.
   (C) Should Buyer furnish false or incomplete information to Seller, Broker(s), or the mortgage lender(s) concerning Buyer's legal or financial status, or fail to cooperate in good faith in processing the mortgage loan application, which results in the mortgage lender(s) refusing to approve a mortgage loan commitment, Buyer will be in default of this Agreement.
   (D) 1. Mortgage commitment date: _____ if Seller does not receive a copy of Buyer's mortgage commitment by this date, Buyer and Seller agree to extend the mortgage commitment date until the Seller terminated this Agreement buy written notice to the Buyer
       2. Upon receiving a mortgage commitment, Buyer will promptly deliver a copy of the commitment to the Seller.
       3. Seller may terminate this Agreement, in writing, after the mortgage commitment date, if the mortgage commitment
          a. is not valid until the date of settlement , OR
          b. is conditional upon the sale and settlement of any other property, OR
          c. does not satisfy all the mortgage terms as stated in paragraph 6(A), OR
          d. Contains any other conditions not specified in this Agreement that is not satisfied and or removed in writing by the mortgage lender(s)
       4. If this Agreement is terminated pursuant to paragraph 6(D)(1) or (3), or the mortgage loan(s) is not obtained for settlement, all deposit monies will be returned to Buyer according to the terms of paragraph 30 and this Agreement will be VOID. Buyer will be responsible for any costs incurred by Buyer for any inspections or certifications obtained according to the terms of this Agreement and any costs incurred by Buyer for (1) Title search, title insurance and or mechanics' lien insurance, or any fee for cancellation. (2) Flood insurance and or fire insurance with extended coverage, mine subsidence insurance or any fee for cancellation (3) Appraisal fee and charges paid in advance to mortgage lender(s)

Figure 6:2 Sample Sales Contract Extraction

4. **FIXTURES & PERSONAL PROPERTY**

(A) INCLUDED in this sale are all existing items, permanently installed in the Property, free of liens, including plumbing, heating, lighting fixtures (including chandeliers and ceiling fans); water treatment systems; pool and spa equipment; garage door openers and transmitters; television antennas; unspotted shrubbery, plantings and trees; any remaining heating and cooking fuels stored on the Property at the time of settlement; sump pumps; storage sheds; mailboxes; wall to wall carpeting; existing window screens, storm windows and screen storm doors, window covering hardware, shades and blinds; awnings; built-in air conditioners, built in appliances; and the range unless otherwise stated. Also included: _____

(B) LEASED items (not owned by Seller): _____

(C) EXCLUDED fixtures and items: _____

_____

Figure 6:9 Sample Sales Contract Extraction

At times, personal property will be included in the sale of real estate. When personal property is to be addressed during the transfer of real property, the details of the items to be excluded or included in the transaction must be outlined specifically within the contract.

The settlement agent should review the inclusions or exclusions written into the sales agreement and confirm that all parties understand and agree to these inclusions or exclusions prior to concluding the settlement meeting.

5. **DATES / TIME IS OF THE ESSENCE**

(A) The settlement date and all other dates and times referred to for the performance of the obligations of this Agreement are of the essence and are binding.

(B) For purposes of this Agreement, the number of days will be counted from the date of execution, excluding the day this Agreement was executed and including the last day of the time period. The Execution Date of this Agreement is the date when Buyer and Seller have indicated full acceptance of this Agreement by signing and/or initialing it. All changes to this Agreement should be initialed and dated.

(C) The settlement date is not extended by any other provision of this Agreement and may only be extended by mutual written Agreement of the parties.

(D) Certain time periods are pre-printed in this Agreement as a convenience to the Buyer and Seller. All pre-printed time periods are negotiable and may be changed by striking out the pre-printed text and inserting a different time period acceptable to all parties.

Figure 6:10 Sample Sales Contract Extraction

When the sales agreement negotiations are finalized, specific dates for action will be incorporated into the contract.

These dates set the timeline expectations for the transaction.

Some dates are listed based upon industry standard expectations and may be open to negotiation such as the term for a pest inspection.

Other dates are negotiated dates between the buyer and the seller and as such are considered fixed dates that must be met.

If a specifically negotiated date cannot be met for any reason, an alteration to the contract, signed by all parties, must be created. This type of date includes items such as the mortgage application and approval dates and the expected close date.

It is very important that the title and settlement company use these dates to set the timeline for the transaction and ensure that all required activity is finalized by the expected close date. Additional details pertaining to the expected time flow of a transaction and potential delays to the closing date are included in a later chapter.

---

6. **MORTGAGE CONTINGENCY**

____ WAIVED This sales is NOT contingent on mortgage financing, although Buyer may still obtain mortgage financing.
____ ELECTED

Figure 6:11 Sample Sales Contract Extraction

When a request to open escrow is received, the individual in charge of the flow of the escrow process should review the sales agreement to determine if there is a mortgage involved in the transaction. If there is a mortgage involved in the transaction, the contingency clause pertaining to mortgage financing may be elected or waived.

When a mortgage lender is involved in the transaction, there may be additional requirements or actions necessary to fund the closing.

If mortgage funds will be used to close the transaction, the settlement company should request all instructions and requirements specific to the loan funding early in the process to ensure that all of the tasks stipulated by the mortgage lender are completed so that the expected close date can be met.

First Mortgage on the Property	**Second Mortgage on the Property**
Loan Amount $_____	Loan Amount $_____
Minimum Term _____ years	Minimum Term _____ years
Type of Mortgage _____	Type of Mortgage _____
Mortgage Lender _____	Mortgage Lender _____
Interest Rate _____% however, Buyer agrees to accept the interest rate as may be committed by the mortgage lender, not to exceed a maximum interest rate of _____%. Discount points, loan origination, loan placement, and other fees charged by the lender as a percentage of the mortgage loan (excluding any mortgage insurance premiums or VA funding fee) not to exceed _____% (1% if not specified)	Interest Rate _____% however, Buyer agrees to accept the interest rate as may be committed by the mortgage lender, not to exceed a maximum interest rate of _____%. Discount points, loan origination, loan placement, and other fees charged by the lender as a percentage of the mortgage loan (excluding any mortgage insurance premiums or VA funding fee) not to exceed _____% (1% if not specified)

Figure 6:12 Sample Sales Contract Extraction

Specific parameters under which the buyer may decline mortgage funding or must accept mortgage funding will often be included in the transaction.

The interest rate(s) and fee(s) provisions in paragraph 6(A) are satisfied if the mortgage lender(s) gives Buyer the right to guarantee the interest rate(s) and fee(s) at or before the maximum levels stated. Buyer gives Seller the right at Seller's sole option and as permitted by law and the mortgage lender(s) to contribute financially, without promise of reimbursement to the buyer and or the mortgage lender(s) to make the above mortgage terms available to the Buyer.

(B) Within _____ days (10 if not specified) from the Execution Date of this Agreement, Buyer will make a completed, written mortgage application for the mortgage terms stated above to the mortgage lender(s) defined in paragraph 6(A), if any, otherwise to a responsible mortgage lender(s) of Buyer's choice. Broker for Buyer, if any, otherwise Broker for Seller, is authorized to communicate with the mortgage lender(s) to assist in the mortgage loan process.

(C) Should Buyer furnish false or incomplete information to Seller, Broker(s), or the mortgage lender(s) concerning Buyer's legal or financial status, or fail to cooperate in good faith in processing the mortgage loan application, which results in the mortgage lender(s) refusing to approve a mortgage loan commitment, Buyer will be in default of this Agreement.

(D) 1. Mortgage commitment date: _____ if Seller does not receive a copy of Buyer's mortgage commitment by this date, Buyer and Seller agree to extend the mortgage commitment date until the Seller terminated this Agreement buy written notice to the Buyer

2. Upon receiving a mortgage commitment, Buyer will promptly deliver a copy of the commitment to the Seller.

3. Seller may terminate this Agreement, in writing, after the mortgage commitment date, if the mortgage commitment
    a. is not valid until the date of settlement , OR
    b. is conditional upon the sale and settlement of any other property, OR
    c. does not satisfy all the mortgage terms as stated in paragraph 6(A), OR
    d. Contains any other conditions not specified in this Agreement that is not satisfied and or removed in writing by the mortgage lender(s)

4. If this Agreement is terminated pursuant to paragraph 6(D)(1) or (3), or the mortgage loan(s) is not obtained for settlement, all deposit monies will be returned to Buyer according to the terms of paragraph 30 and this Agreement will be VOID. Buyer will be responsible for any costs incurred by Buyer for any inspections or certifications obtained according to the terms of this Agreement and any costs incurred by Buyer for (1) Title search, title insurance and or mechanics' lien insurance, or any fee for cancellation. (2) Flood insurance and or fire insurance with extended coverage, mine subsidence insurance or any fee for cancellation (3) Appraisal fee and charges paid in advance to mortgage lender(s)

Figure 6:13 Sample Sales Contract Extraction

Timelines for application and approval of mortgage funding will be included in the contract. These dates will assist you in setting the time flow and activity sheets for the closing preparations you must undertake to meet the expected close date.

Additional details that may be applicable to your transaction such as costs, fees and other matters may be incorporated. Any detail included within the sales agreement under the mortgage contingency clause should be transferred to your escrow sheet.

Additional details as to how you will interpret and use mortgage instructions and parameters are included in a later chapter.

REAL ESTATE CLOSING - SETTLEMENT AGENT

(E) If the mortgage lender(s), or an insurer providing property and casualty insurance s required by the mortgage lender(s), requires repairs to the Property, Buyer will, upon receiving the requirements, deliver a copy of the requirements to the Seller. Within ___ DAYS of receiving the copy of the requirements, Seller will notify Buyer whether Seller will make the required repairs at Seller's expense.

    1. If Seller makes the required repairs to the satisfaction of the mortgage lender(s) or insurer, Buyer accepts the Property and agrees to the RELEASE in paragraph 27 of this Agreement.

    2. If Seller will not make the required repairs, or if Seller fails to respond within the time given, Buyer will, within ___ days, notify Seller of Buyer's choice to:

      a. Make the required repairs, at Buyer's expense, with permission and access to the Property given by Seller; permission and access may not be unreasonably withheld by Seller, OR

      b. Terminate this Agreement by written notice to Seller, with all deposit monies returned to Buyer according to the terms of paragraph 30 of this Agreement.

(F) **Seller Assist**

  ___ NOT APPLICABLE

  ___ APPLICABLE, Seller will pay:

    $_____, or _____% of Purchase Price, maximum, toward Buyer's costs as acceptable to the mortgage lender(s)

FHA/VA, IF APPLIABLE

(G) It is expressly agreed that notwithstanding any other provisions of this contract, Buyer will not be obligated to complete the purchase of the Property described herein or to incur any penalty by forfeiture of earnest money deposits or otherwise unless Buyer has been given, in accordance with HUD/FHA or VA requirements, a written statement by the Federal Housing Commissioner, Veterans Administration, or a Direct Endorsement Lender setting forth the appraised value of the Property of not less than $_____ (the dollar amount to be inserted is the sales price as stated in this Agreement). Buyer will have the privilege and option of proceeding with consummation of the contract without regard to the amount of the appraised valuation. The appraised valuation is arrived at to determine the maximum mortgage the Department of Housing and Urban Development will insure. HUD does not warrant the value nor the condition of the Property as acceptable.

  Warning: Section 1010 of Title 18, U.S.C., Department of Housing and Urban Development and Federal Housing Administration Transactions, provides, "Whoever for the purpose of…influencing in any way the action of such Department, makes, passes, utters or publishes any statement, knowing the same to be false… shall be fined under this title or imprisoned not more than two years or both."

(H) **U.S. Department of Housing and Urban Development (HUD) NOTICE TO PURCHASERS: Buyer's Acknowledgement**

  ___ Buyer has received the HUD Notice "For Your Protection: Get a Home Inspection." Buyer understands the importance of getting an independent home inspection and has thought about this before signing this Agreement. Buyer understands that FHA will not perform a home inspection nor guarantee the price or condition of the Property.

(I) **Certification** We the undersigned, Seller(s) and Buyer(s) party to this transaction each certify that the terms of this contract for purchase are true to the best of our knowledge and believe, and that any other agreement entered into by any of these parties in connection with this transaction is attached to this Agreement.

7. **WAIVER OF CONTINGENCIES**
If this Agreement is contingent on Buyer's right to inspect and/or repair the Property, or to verify insurability, environmental conditions, boundaries, certifications, zoning classification or use, or any other information regarding the Property, Buyer's failure to exercise any of Buyer's options within the times set forth in this Agreement is a WAIVER of that contingency and Buyer accepts the Property and agrees to the RELEASE in paragraph 27 of this Agreement.

8. **PROPERTY INSURANCE AVAILABILITY**
  ___ WAIVED. This Agreement is NOT contingent upon Buyer obtaining property and casualty insurance for the Property, although Buyer may still obtain property and casualty insurance.
  ___ ELECTED. Contingency Period: ___ DAYS (15 if not specified) from the Execution Date of this Agreement.
  Within the Contingency Period, Buyer will make application for property and casualty insurance for the Property to a responsible insurer. **Broker for Buyer, if any, otherwise Broker for Seller, may communicate with the insurer to assist in the insurance process**. If Buyer cannot obtain property and casualty insurance for the Property on terms and conditions reasonably acceptable to Buyer, Buyer will, within the Contingency Period:
  (A) Accept the Property and agree to the RELEASE in paragraph 27 of this Agreement, OR
  (B) Terminate this Agreement by written notice to Seller, with all deposit monies returned to Buyer according to the terms of paragraph 30 of this Agreement, OR
  (C) Enter into a mutually acceptable written agreement with Seller.
  If Buyer and Seller do not reach a written agreement during the Contingency Period, and Buyer does not terminate this Agreement by written notice to Seller within that time, Buyer will accept the Property and agree to the RELEASE in paragraph 27 of this Agreement.

9. **INSPECTIONS**
  (A) Seller will provide access to insurers' representatives and, as may be required by this Agreement, to surveyors, municipal officials, and inspectors. If Buyer is obtaining mortgage financing, Seller will provide access to the Property to appraisers and others reasonably required by the mortgage lender(s). Buyer may attend any inspections.

Figure 6:14 Sample Sales Contract Page 3

(E)   If the mortgage lender(s), or an insurer providing property and casualty insurance s required by the mortgage lender(s), requires repairs to the Property, Buyer will, upon receiving the requirements, deliver a copy of the requirements to the Seller. Within ___ DAYS of receiving the copy of the requirements, Seller will notify Buyer whether Seller will make the required repairs at Seller's expense.

      1.   If Seller makes the required repairs to the satisfaction of the mortgage lender(s) or insurer, Buyer accepts the Property and agrees to the RELEASE in paragraph 27 of this Agreement.

      2.   If Seller will not make the required repairs, or if Seller fails to respond within the time given, Buyer will, within ___ days, notify Seller of Buyer's choice to:

      a.   Make the required repairs, at Buyer's expense, with permission and access to the Property given by Seller; permission and access may not be unreasonably withheld by Seller, OR

      b.   Terminate this Agreement by written notice to Seller, with all deposit monies returned to Buyer according to the terms of paragraph 30 of this Agreement.

Figure 6:15 Sample Sales Contract Extraction

At times, the mortgage lender or property insurance company chosen by the buyer will require that specific repairs be made to the property being transferred. When this occurs, the negotiation as to who will make such repairs may become an issue in moving forward with the settlement. Some real estate contracts will opt to negotiate the specifics of such repairs before any inspections are made. These specifics will be detailed within the contract.

If such negotiations exist, the results from a failure on the part of the named responsible party to make such repairs will be detailed. These details could include the rights of the other party to cancel the transaction without penalty, to make said repairs themselves and charge, or not to charge the other party for said repairs.

The time allocation for all applicable actions will also be detailed. The time period named could become an important issue to the settlement agent in that required repairs could slow the transaction flow and result in an extension of the expected closing date.

(F)   **Seller Assist**
   __   NOT APPLICABLE
   __   APPLICABLE, Seller will pay:
      $_____, or _____% of Purchase Price, maximum, toward Buyer's costs as acceptable to the mortgage lender(s)

Figure 6:16 Sample Sales Contract Extraction

The practice of requesting assistance toward the payment of closing costs from the seller in a transaction is becoming more common.

Many standard real estate sales agreements have incorporated a specific clause pertaining to this negotiation.

Seller concessions are the specific amount of funds a seller will allocate toward paying a buyer's closing costs out of the seller's closing proceeds.

Many mortgage lenders have maximum amounts of seller assistance that they will allow.

If seller assistance is incorporated into the sales agreement, you should note the negotiated details on your escrow sheet and then verify the applicable parameters set by the mortgage lender.

Seller assistance amounts will be incorporated in to the HUD 1 and will often be clearly defined within the instructions received for closing from the Mortgage Lender.

You should verify all of the seller assistance details, allowed costs offsets and inclusion of such assistance on the HUD 1 prior to beginning the settlement meeting.

Many borrowers require assistance in obtaining all of the required funds for closing and seller assistance is one tool that will enable the borrower to secure adequate funds. It is important that you understand that seller assistance funds come from the transaction. What this means is that the funds appear as a credit from the seller, but the money used will actually come from the loan funds and down payment money that the borrower brings to the table.

You should verify all of the seller assistance details, allowed costs offsets, and the inclusion of such assistance on the HUD 1 prior to beginning the settlement meeting. All of the entries relating to closing cost assistance must comply with the requirements of the loan guidelines. If any wording or allocation agreement relating to the closing cost assistance does not meet the requirements of the loan guidelines, the sales agreement will need to be modified to bring the negotiations into line with the mortgage approval terms.

At times, errors in the calculations or application of the seller assistance funds can occur during the preparation of the closing documents. It is important that all allowable seller assistance be credited to the borrower at the closing and that the assistance is credited in the correct location on the HUD 1.

Example: The loan guidelines dictate that the seller assistance may be applied to non-recurring closing costs, the allocation of seller assistance on the HUD 1 must be in entries related to non-recurring closing costs.

If the closing agent preparing the settlement statement was to enter some of the seller assistance money in the area detailing payment for homeowners insurance a problem may arise that delays the closing.

Homeowner's insurance premiums are recurring closing costs.

The entry of the seller assistance funds in this area may cause underwriting to invalidate the transaction until the funds are applied according to the guidelines.

The ability to review all documentation before the commencement of closing will enable you to isolate and correct issues before the parties arrive to close the transaction. Gaining a reputation for processing loan packages that lead to a smooth closing is one element that will assist you in growing your business and ensuring referral business from each loan that you close.

Certain specific inspections of the property may be written into the agreement. It is important for you to know some basic facts pertaining to these inspections. You will need to locate the

- Information detailing who will pay for the inspection

- And the specific agreement regarding when the payment for the inspections will be made

The payment for any required inspections may be made outside of closing or these payments may become part of the closing costs paid at the settlement meeting.

All billings pertaining to the transaction that are not paid prior to close must be addressed at the closing table so that the transaction may close without additional obligations coming to the surface for either the buyer or the seller at some point in the future.

When inspections are completed, specific items may become known that must be addressed or corrected prior to the closing of the loan.

Example: If a termite inspection is completed and termites are found on the subject property, one party will likely be responsible for having the problems relating to the termites corrected.

This could cause closing delays while the problem is corrected.

Any matter that must be corrected may also result in additional costs.

The handling of deficiencies should be written into the contracts and all inspections should be ordered early in the loan process. Addressing these items early helps to ensure that there is adequate time to remedy any issues that are discovered.

10. INSPECTION CONTINGENCY OPTIONS

The inspection contingencies elected by Buyer in paragraphs 11-15 are controlled by the Options set forth below. The time periods in these Options will apply to all inspection contingencies in paragraphs 11-15 unless otherwise stated in this Agreement.

Option 1. Within the Contingency Period, as stated in paragraphs 11-15, Buyer will:

1. Accept the Property with the information stated in the report(s) and agree to the RELEASE in paragraph 27 of this Agreement, OR
2. If Buyer is not satisfied with the information stated in the report(s), terminate this Agreement by written notice to the Seller, with all deposit monies returned to the Buyer according to the terms of paragraph 30 of this Agreement, OR
3. Enter into a mutually acceptable written agreement with the Seller providing for any repairs or improvements to the Property and or any credit to Buyer at settlement, as acceptable to the mortgage lender(s), if any.

   If Buyer and Seller do not reach a written agreement during the specified Contingency Period, and Buyer does not terminate this Agreement by written notice to Seller within that time, Buyer will accept the Property and agree to the RELEASE in paragraph 27 of this Agreement.

Option 2. Within the Contingency Period, as stated in paragraphs 11-15, Buyer will:

1. Accept the Property with the information stated in the report(s) and agree to the RELEASE in paragraph 27 of this Agreement, OR
2. If Buyer is not satisfied with the information stated in the report(s), present the report(s) to Seller with a Written Corrective Proposal ("Proposal") listing corrections and/or credits desired by Buyer. The Proposal may, but is not required to, include the name of a properly licensed or qualified professional to perform the corrections requested in the Proposal, provisions for payment, including retests, and a projected date for completion of the corrections. Buyer agrees that Seller will not be held liable for corrections that do not comply with mortgage lender or governmental requirements if performed in a workmanlike manner according to the terms of Buyer's Proposal, or by a contractor selected by Buyer.

   a. Within ___ days (7 if not specified) of receiving Buyer's Proposal, Seller will inform Buyer in writing of Seller's choice to:
   1. Satisfy the terms of Buyer's Proposal, OR
   2. Credit Buyer at settlement for the cost to satisfy the terms of Buyer's Proposal, as acceptable to mortgage lender(s), if any, OR
   3. Not satisfy the terms of Buyer's Proposal or to credit Buyer at settlement for the costs to satisfy the terms of Buyer's Proposal.

   b. If Seller agrees to satisfy the terms of Buyer's Proposal or to credit Buyer at settlement as specified above, Buyer accepts Property and agrees to the RELEASE in paragraph 27 of this Agreement.

   c. If seller chooses not to satisfy the terms of Buyer's Proposal and not to credit Buyer at settlement as specified above, of if Seller fails to choose any option within the time give, Buyer will within ___ days (5 if not specified);
   1. Accept the Property with the information stated in the report(s) and agree to the RELEASE in paragraph 27 of this Agreement, OR
   2. Terminate this Agreement by written notice to Seller, with all deposit monies returned to Buyer according to the terms of paragraph 30 of this Agreement, OR
   3. Enter into a mutually acceptable written agreement with Seller providing for any repairs or improvements to the Property and/or any credit to Buyer at settlement, as acceptable to the mortgage lender(s) if any.

11. **PROPERTY INSPECTION CONTINGENCY** (See Property and Environmental Inspection Notices)

Buyer understands that property inspections, certifications and/or investigations can be performed by professional contractors, home inspectors, engineers, architects and other properly licensed or otherwise qualified professionals, and may include, but are not limited to: structural components; roof; exterior windows and exterior doors; exterior siding, fascia, gutters and downspouts; swimming pools, hot tubs and spas; appliances; electrical, plumbing, heating and cooling systems; water penetration; environmental hazards (e.g., mold, fungi, indoor air quality, asbestos, underground storage tanks, etc.); electromagnetic fields; wetlands inspection; flood plain verification; property boundary/square footage verification; and any other items Buyer may select. Buyer is advised to investigate easements, deed and use restrictions (including any historic preservation restrictions or ordinances) that apply to the Property and to review local zoning ordinances. Other provisions of this Agreement may provide for inspections, certifications and/or investigations that are not waived or altered by Buyer's election here.

___ WAIVED Buyer has the option to conduct property inspections, certifications, and/or investigations. Buyer WAIVES THIS OPTION and agrees to the RELEASE in paragraph 27 of this agreement.

___ ELECTED Contingency Period: ___ days (15 if not specified) from the Execution Date of this Agreement.

(A) Within the Contingency Period, Buyer, at Buyer's expense, may have inspections, certifications and/or investigations completed by properly licensed or otherwise qualified professionals. If Buyer elects to have a home inspection of the Property, as defined in the Pennsylvania Home Inspection Law (see Information Regarding the Home Inspection Law), the home inspection must be performed by a full member of a national home inspection association, in accordance with the ethical standards and code of conduct or practice of that association, or by a properly licensed or registered professional engineer, or a properly licensed or registered architect. This contingency does not apply to the following conditions or items: _____

(B) If Buyer is not satisfied with the condition of the Property as stated in the written inspection report(s), Buyer will proceed under one of the following Options as listed in paragraph 10 within the Contingency Period:

___ Option 1

___ Option 2 For the purposes of Paragraph 11 only, Buyer agrees to accept the Property with the results of any report(s) and agrees to the RELEASE in paragraph 27 of this Agreement if the total cost to correct the conditions stated in the report(s) is less than $_____ ($0 if not specified) (the "Deductible Amount"). Otherwise, all provisions of paragraph 10, Option 2, shall apply, except that Seller will be deemed to have satisfied the terms of Buyer's Proposal if Seller agrees to perform corrections or offer credits such that the cumulative cost of any uncorrected or uncredited condition(s) is equal to the Deductible Amount.

Figure 6:17 Sample Sales Contract Page 5

KENNEY

2. WOOD INFESTATION INSPECTION CONTINGENCY

___ WAIVED. Buyer has the option to have the Property inspected for wood infestation by an inspector certified as a wood-destroying pest pesticide applicator. BUYER WAIVES THIS OPTOIN and agrees to the RELEASE in paragraph 27 of this Agreement.

___ ELECTED. Contingency Period ___ days (15 if not specified) from the Execution Date of this Agreement.

(A) Within the Contingency Period, Buyer, at Buyer's expense, may obtain a written "Wood Destroying Insect Infestation Inspection Report" from an inspector certified as a wood-destroying pests pesticide applicator and will deliver it an all supporting documents and drawings provided by the inspector to Seller. The report is to be made satisfactory to and in compliance with applicable laws, mortgage lender requirements, and/or Federal Insuring and Guaranteeing Agency requirements, if any. The inspection is to be limited to all readily visible and accessible areas of all structures on the Property except fences and the following structures, which will not be inspected:

_____

(B) If the inspection reveals active infestation(s), Buyer, at Buyer's expense, may within the Contingency Period, obtain a proposal from a wood-destroying pest pesticide applicator to treat the Property.

(C) If the inspection reveals damage from active or previous infestation(s), Buyer, at Buyer's expense, may within the Contingency Period, obtain a written report from a professional contractor, home inspector, or structural engineer that is limited to structural damage to the Property caused by wood-destroying organisms and a Proposal to repair and/or treat the Property.

(D) If Buyer is not satisfied with the condition of the Property as stated in the written inspection report(s), Buyer will proceed under one of the following Options as listed in paragraph 10 within the Contingency Period:
___ Option 1
___ Option 2

3. STATUS OF RADON

(A) Seller has no knowledge concerning the presence or absence of radon unless checked below:

___ 1. Seller has knowledge that the Property was tested on the dates, by the methods (e.g., charcoal canister, alpha track, etc.), and with the results of the test indicated below:
DATE   TYPE OF TEST   RESULTS (picocuries/liter or working levels)
_____

___ 2. Seller has knowledge that the Property underwent radon reduction measures on the date(s) and by the method(s) indicated below:
DATE   RADON REDUCTION METHOD
_____

COPIES OF ALL AVAILABLE TEST REPORTS will be delivered to Buyer with this Agreement. SELLER DOES NOT WARRANT EITHER THE METHODS OR RESULTS OF THE TESTS.

(B) RADON INSPECTION CONTINGENCY

___ WAIVED. Buyer has the option to have the Property inspected for radon by a certified inspector. BUYER WAIVES THIS OPTION and agrees to the RELEASE in paragraph 27 of this Agreement.

___ ELECTED. Contingency Period: ___ Days (15 if not specified) from the Execution Date of this Agreement.
Within the Contingency Period, Buyer, at Buyer's expense, may obtain a radon test a radon test of the Property from a certified inspector. If Seller performs any radon remediation, Seller will provide Buyer a certification that the remediation was performed by a properly licensed and certified radon mitigation company.

1. If the written test report reveals the presence of radon below 0.02 working levels or 4 picoCuries/liter(4 pCi/L), Buyer accepts the Property and agrees to the RELEASE in paragraph 27 of this Agreement.

2. If the written test report reveals the presence of radon at or exceeding 0.02 working levels or 4 picoCuries/liter (4 pCi/L), Buyer will proceed under one of the following options as listed in paragraph 10 within the Contingency Period.
___ Option 1
___ Option 2

4. STAUTS OF WATER

(A) Seller represents that the Property is served by:
___ Public Water
___ On-site Water
___ Community Water
___ None
_____

(B) WATER SERVICE INSPECTION CONTINGENCY

___ WAIVED. Buyer has the option to have an inspection of the quality and or quantity of the water system for the Property. BUYER WAIVES THIS OPTION and agrees to the RELEASE in paragraph 27 of this Agreement.

___ ELECTED. Contingency Period ___ days (15 if not specified) from the Execution Date of this Agreement.

1. Within the Contingency Period, Buyer, at Buyer's expense, may obtain an inspection of the quality and/or quantity of the water system from a properly licensed or otherwise qualified water/well testing company.

2. If required by the inspection company, Seller, at Seller's expense, will locate and provide access to the on-site (or individual) water system. Seller also agrees to restore the Property, at Seller's expense, prior to settlement.

3. If Buyer is not satisfied with the condition of the water system as stated in the written inspection report(s), Buyer will proceed under one of the following options as listed in paragraph 10 within the Contingency Period:
___ Option 1
___ Option 2

Figure 6:18 Sample Sales Contract Page 5

Certain specific inspections of the property may be written into the agreement. It is important for you to know some basic facts pertaining to these inspections.

- Information detailing who will pay for the inspection

- When the payment will be made

The payment for any required inspections may be made outside of closing or these payments may become part of the closing costs listed on the settlement statement.

All billings pertaining to the transaction that are not paid prior to close must be addressed at the closing table so that the transaction may close without additional obligations coming to the surface for either the buyer or the seller at some point in the future.

When inspections are completed, specific items may become known that must be addressed or corrected prior to the closing of the loan.

Example: If a termite inspection is completed and termites are found on the subject property, one party will likely be responsible for having the problems relating to the termites corrected.

This could cause closing delays while the problem is corrected.

Any matter that must be corrected may also result in additional costs.

The handling of deficiencies should be written into the contracts you receive when escrow was opened.

If such inspections are ordered and the remedy processes are not included, you will want to confirm the handling of any issues that may arise.

(C)   In the event any notices (including violations) and/or assessments are received after Seller has signed this Agreement and before settlement, Seller will provide a copy of the notices and/or assessments to Buyer and will notify Buyer in writing within ___ days after receiving the notices and/or assessments that seller will:

    1. Fully comply with the notices and/or assessments at Seller's expense before settlement. If Seller fully complies with the notices and/or assessments, Buyer accepts the Property and agrees to the RELEASE in paragraph 27 of this Agreement OR

    2. Not comply with the notices and/or assessments. If Seller chooses not to comply with the notices and/or assessments, or fails within the time given to notify Buyer whether Seller will comply, Buyer will notify Seller in writing within ___ days that Buyer will:

        a.   Comply with the notices and/or assessments at Buyer's expense, accept the Property, and agree to the RELEASE in paragraph 27 of this Agreement OR

        b.   Terminate this Agreement by written notice to Seller, with all deposit monies returned to Buyer according to the terms of paragraph 30 of this Agreement.

        If Buyer fails to respond within the time stated in paragraph 18 (C) (2) or fails to terminate this Agreement by written notice to the Seller within that time, Buyer will accept the Property and agree to the RELEASE in paragraph 27 of this Agreement.

(D)   If required by law, within ___ DAYS From the Execution Date of this Agreement, but in no case later than 15 days prior to settlement, Seller will order at Seller's expense a certification from the appropriate municipal department(s) disclosing notice of any uncorrected violations of zoning, housing, building, safety, or fire ordinances and/or a certificate permitting occupancy of the Property. If Buyer receives notice of any required repairs/improvements, Buyer will promptly deliver a copy of the notice to the Seller.

    1. Within ___ DAYS of receiving notice form the municipality that repairs/improvements are required, Seller will notify Buyer in writing that the Seller will:

        a.   Make the required repairs/improvements to the satisfaction of the municipality. If Seller makes the require repairs/improvements, Buyer accepts the Property and agrees to the RELEASE in paragraph 27 of this Agreement OR

        b.   Not make the required repairs/improvements. If Seller chooses not to make the required repairs/improvements, Buyer will notify Seller in writing within ___ DAYS that Buyer will:

            (1)   Make the repairs/improvements at Buyer's expense, with permission and access to the Property given by Seller, which will not be unreasonably withheld, OR

            (2)   Terminate this Agreement by written notice to Seller, with all deposit monies returned to Buyer according to the terms of paragraph 30 of this Agreement.

        If Buyer fails to respond within the time stated in paragraph 18 (D) (1) (b) or fails to terminate this Agreement by written notice to Seller within that time, Buyer will accept the Property and agree to the RELEASE in paragraph 27 of this Agreement, and Buyer accepts the responsibility to perform the repairs/improvements according to the terms of the notice provided by the municipality.

    2. If Seller denies Buyer permission to make the required repairs/improvements, or does not provide Buyer access before settlement to make the required repairs/improvements, Buyer may, within ___ DAYS, terminate this Agreement by written notice to Seller, with all deposit monies returned to Buyer according to paragraph 30 of this Agreement

    3. If repairs/improvements are required and Seller fails to provide a copy of the notice to Buyer as required in paragraph 18 (D), Seller will perform all repairs/improvements as required by the notice at Seller's expense. Paragraph 18(D)(3) will survive settlement.

19.   TITLE, SURVEYS & COSTS

(A)   The Property will be conveyed with good and marketable title as is insurable by a reputable title company at the regular rates, free and clear of all liens, encumbrances, and easements, EXCEPTING HOWEVER the following: existing deed restrictions; historic preservation restrictions or ordinances; building restrictions; ordinances; easements of roads; easements visible upon the ground; easements of record; and privileges or rights of public service companies, if any.

(B)   Buyer will pay for the following: (1) Title search, title insurance and/or mechanics' lien insurance, or any fee for cancellation; (2) Flood insurance, fire insurance with extended coverage, mine subsidence insurance, or any fee for cancellation; (3) Appraisal fees and charges paid in advance to mortgage lender(s); (4) Buyer's customary settlement costs and accruals.

(C)   Any survey or surveys required by the title insurance company or abstracting attorney for preparing an adequate legal description of the Property (or the correction thereof) will be obtained and paid for by Seller. Any survey or surveys desired by Buyer or required by the mortgage lender will be obtained and paid for by Buyer.

(D)   If Seller is unable to give a good and marketable title and such as is insurable by a reputable title insurance company at the regular rates, as specified in paragraph 19 (A), Buyer will:

    1. Accept the Property with such title as Seller can give, with no change to the purchase price, and agree to the RELEASE in paragraph 27 of this Agreement, OR

    2. Terminate this Agreement by written notice to Seller, with all deposit monies to Buyer according to the terms of paragraph 30 of this Agreement. Upon termination, Seller will reimburse Buyer for any costs incurred by Buyer for any inspections or certifications obtained according to the terms of this Agreement, and for those items specified in paragraph 19 (B) items (1), (2), (3) and in paragraph 19 (C).

(E)   The property is not a "recreational cabin" as defined in the Pennsylvania Construction Code Act unless otherwise stated here (see information regarding Recreational Cabins): _____

20.   CONDOMINIUM/PLANNED COMMUNITY (HOMEOWNER ASSOCIATION) RESALE NOTICE

  __   NOT APPLICABLE

  __   APPLICABLE

Figure 6:19 Sample Sales Contract Extraction

19. TITLE, SURVEYS & COSTS

(A) The Property will be conveyed with good and marketable title as is insurable by a reputable title company at the regular rates, free and clear of all liens, encumbrances, and easements, EXCEPTING HOWEVER the following: existing deed restrictions; historic preservation restrictions or ordinances; building restrictions; ordinances; easements of roads; easements visible upon the ground; easements of record; and privileges or rights of public service companies, if any.

(B) Buyer will pay for the following: (1) Title search, title insurance and/or mechanics' lien insurance, or any fee for cancellation; (2) Flood insurance, fire insurance with extended coverage, mine subsidence insurance, or any fee for cancellation; (3) Appraisal fees and charges paid in advance to mortgage lender(s); (4) Buyer's customary settlement costs and accruals.

(C) Any survey or surveys required by the title insurance company or abstracting attorney for preparing an adequate legal description of the Property (or the correction thereof) will be obtained and paid for by Seller. Any survey or surveys desired by Buyer or required by the mortgage lender will be obtained and paid for by Buyer.

(D) If Seller is unable to give a good and marketable title and such as is insurable by a reputable title insurance company at the regular rates, as specified in paragraph 19 (A), Buyer will:

1. Accept the Property with such title as Seller can give, with no change to the purchase price, and agree to the RELEASE in paragraph 27 of this Agreement, OR

2. Terminate this Agreement by written notice to Seller, with all deposit monies to Buyer according to the terms of paragraph 30 of this Agreement. Upon termination, Seller will reimburse Buyer for any costs incurred by Buyer for any inspections or certifications obtained according to the terms of this Agreement, and for those items specified in paragraph 19 (B) items (1), (2), (3) and in paragraph 19 (C).

(E) The property is not a "recreational cabin" as defined in the Pennsylvania Construction Code Act unless otherwise stated here (see information regarding Recreational Cabins): _____

Figure 6:21 Sample Sales Contract Extraction

Specific terms relating to

- The marketability of the title

- The ability to insure the title

- Restrictions specific to the property

- Easements, rights and privileges pertaining to the property

- The costs pertaining to the searching and insuring the title

- Survey completion and costs

may be incorporated into the sales agreement. If any item cannot be met according to the contract, the options available to the parties should be outlined.

These terms should be verified by the settlement agent, specifically those relating to the party who will bear the costs associated with each of these contingency clauses. If any question exists pertaining to which party will pay for the costs associated with any clause, you should contact the buyer, seller or real estate agent to obtain a formalized agreement between the parties prior to completing the HUD 1 or beginning the settlement meeting.

23. POSSESSION
   (A) Possession is to be delivered by deed, keys and:
   1. Physical possession to vacant Property free of debris, with all structures broom-clean at day and time of settlement, AND/OR
   2. Assignment of any existing lease(s), together with any security deposits and interest, at day and time of settlement, if Property is leased at the execution of this Agreement, unless otherwise stated in this Agreement.
   (B) Buyer will acknowledge existing lease(s) by initialing the lease(s) at the execution of this Agreement, unless otherwise specified herein.
   (C) Seller will not enter into any new leases, extensions of existing leases or additional leases for the Property without the written consent of Buyer.

Figure 6:23 Sample Sales Contract Extraction

Details regarding possession of the property as well as any lease assignments relating to the property should be incorporated into the sales agreement. Many standard agreements contain a clause that provides default instructions for a transaction. Any alteration to this clause would appear in an addendum to the contract. The settlement agent should confirm the specific negotiations pertaining to possession to make certain that all contractually negotiated pre-requisites are complete prior to beginning the settlement meeting. If possession is to occur at some point in the future or based upon an unusual negotiation, the settlement agent should verify that all parties understand the process for possession prior to concluding the meeting.

If the property is currently leased, the handling of lease assignments will often occur at the closing. The settlement agent should confirm the time stated for the transfer of lease agreements, the method of prorating lease funds and transferring escrowed security deposits prior to beginning the settlement meeting. You should also confirm that all actions pertaining to the lease agreements are completed prior to concluding the meeting.

30. TERMINATION & RETURN OF DEPOSITS
   (A) Where Buyer terminates this Agreement pursuant to any right granted by this Agreement, all deposit monies paid on account of purchase will be returned to the buyer and this agreement will be VOID. The broker holding the deposit monies may only release the deposit monies according to the terms of a fully executed written agreement between Buyer and Seller ands as permitted by the rules and regulations of the State Real Estate Commission

   (B) If there is a dispute over entitlement to deposit monies, a broker is not legally permitted to determine if a breach occurred or which party is entitled to deposit monies. A broker holding monies is required by the Rules and Regulations of the State Real Estate Commission to retain the monies in escrow until the dispute is resolved. In the event of litigation over deposit monies, a broker will distribute monies according to the terms of a final order of court or a written agreement of the parties. Buyer and Seller agree that, if any broker or affiliated licensee is joined in litigation regarding deposit monies, the attorney's fees and costs of the broker(s) and licensee(s) will be paid by the party joining them.

Figure 6:25 Sample Sales Contract Extraction

Details regarding the earnest money deposit, the application of the deposit toward costs and the specifics of how or when the buyer may regain or loose rights to the earnest money deposited should be outlined within the contract.

Standard contracts typically contain a specific clause dealing with the earnest money deposit, but these standard clauses can be altered through additions to the contract or by addendums to the sales agreement. Non-standard contracts should specify the pertinent handling of earnest money funds.

If a contract for an escrow you are handling does not, the individual responsible for preparing the transaction for closing should obtain written specifics signed by the buyer and seller with regard to the application of the earnest money funds.

STATEMENT OF ESTIMATED SELLER'S COSTS

Date Prepared   Sellers
Prepared By   Property

The following estimate is given so that the Sellers will understand approximately what costs will be deducted from the proceeds of the sale at the time of settlement.

		Sales Price	$
1.)	Deed Preparation		$
2.)	Settlement Fee		$
3.)	State ___ % Transfer Tax		$
4.)	Local ___ % Transfer Tax		$
5.)	Broker Fee		$
Total Cost To Seller			$
Net Amount To Seller			$

I/We understand that this is only an estimate of My/Our costs relative to the sale of _____ No consideration has been given for Pro-Rated Taxes, Water and Sewage, or Balance Due on Mortgage if any. I/We understand that this in only an estimate of my/our costs and acknowledge receipt of a copy of the statement of Estimated Seller's Costs.

Figure 6:6 Statement of Estimated Sellers Costs Example

Commissions   The sales agreement will typically outline any commission funds to be paid to the Real Estate Agent, Mortgage Lender or other party.

These commission payments are often paid at the close of escrow and you should confirm such inclusions and that the applicable amounts are included within the settlement statement.

The Real Estate Agent will often provide the seller with an estimate of their costs in the transaction at the time the real estate purchase agreement is finalized. These are only estimates and may or may not be the same as the data included on the HUD 1.

You should verify the costs assessed to the seller through entries on the sales contract, any addendums and any additional negotiated documents that contain the signatures of both parties as these will be more exact and will more accurately reflect the final figures associated with the transaction.

Sale Contingency

At times, the buyer may need to sell another property to gain the funds needed to close or the seller may need to locate another property in order to provide possession of the subject property to the buyer.

If another property is involved in the transaction, details relating to these other properties and the actions that must occur will often be written into the sales agreement. You should confirm whether such contingencies exist and maintain information regarding the progress. Such a contingency may affect the expected closing date.

Example: If the buyer must sell another property in order to close on the subject property, closing may be delayed if the market conditions for the sale of the buyers other home are slow.

The handling of such a delay will often be outlined within the expected closing date clause.

Any delay will affect your timeline and may result in a cancellation of the entire transaction.

Other conditions or contingencies may be written into the sales agreement. Any item that is of concern or interest to either party may become part of the agreement for transfer. You should review the entire contract, addendums and other paperwork remitted to your office to gain a better understanding of the unique applications in each transaction. As you can see, the specifics of the transaction will alter the methodology, specifics and handling of the closing and so gaining a complete understanding of each potential alteration will benefit you by making closings a smoother process for all parties.

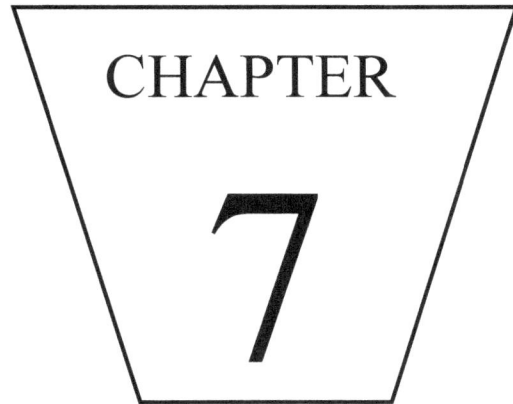

CHAPTER

7

TITLE SEARCH

An abstract of title is the summary of all recorded documents filed within the public records system that apply to a particular parcel of land. The abstract summary recites all matters that may impede the right of a property owner to the full enjoyment of his land. The abstract is a critical element in the closing process in that it confirms the ability of the seller to transfer the property to the buyer under the conditions that are negotiated within the sales contract.

After escrow has been opened with an escrow order and the timeline has been set, the title search process will begin. The company for which you work may or may not provide title search services.

- If you work for a closing company only, the title search may be completed by another company and only the commitments and insurance will be given to you at the closing.

- If your company completes the title search and assists in the issuance of insurance, you will have knowledge of any search issues that come up during the process.

Regardless of who handles the title search and insurance issuance, you should gain a basic understanding of the actions that will occur during the process. The title search process is very detailed and many matters may exist that are addressed during the search, commitment and insurance processes.

If you wish to gain a complete understanding of the processes and actions that occur during a title search, commitment and insurance process, coursework is available that provides training pertaining to all of the functions of an abstractor and title company. For now, we will provide you with a basic understanding of the processes that occur outside of your functions and how they may affect the potential closing you will handle.

A title search is the research conducted to trace the chain of title on a piece of property back in time through the public records system. The primary focus of the title search is to confirm that the individual offering the property for sale actually has complete ownership of the property and what defects, if any, exist within the chain of title.

The abstractor or title searcher will search all records on file for public review that pertain to the piece of property being transferred as well as certain records pertaining to the individual offering the property for sale. These will include such locations as the county recorders office, the county assessor's office, other taxing agency records and any pendens indexes among other records specific to the property or seller.

These records will be reviewed to locate any and all documents, actions or inactions that might affect the title to the subject property. The abstractor will locate specifics of the property such as

- the exact description

- the estate or interest held by the seller of the property

- any exceptions such as liens, encumbrances or other defects that exist in relationship to the subject property

- any items or actions taken against the property owner that might impact the title to the property

- any other matter that appears in public record with an applicability to the transaction may require additional research and become part of the title commitment, exceptions or insurance issuances

The title will be searched through every transfer backward in time that relates to the specific property. If any defect is located, it will be noted on the preliminary title report and may become a matter that must be cured or corrected prior to close or it may become a matter that is excepted within the title insurance policy.

- If the matter must be cured, additional delays in the closing process may occur while the matter is addressed.

- If the matter is to be excepted in the title insurance policy, then the buyers must be aware that they are making the purchase of the property with specific defects attached.

Example: An individual who once owned all or a portion of the property failed to pay the required inheritance tax when the property transferred from a parent to them, a child.

If such a tax was not paid at the time of transfer, the proper payment will be considered a lien against the property and should be addressed prior to transferring the property during closing.

Example: A restriction against specific actions or use at the subject property might exist.

Deeds will sometimes contain restrictions as to what an individual owner may or may not do with their property.

Any restriction in any deed throughout the chain of title that has not been expressly released by the individual or representative of the individual placing the restriction will affect the buyer's ability to use the property in certain ways.

Example: No signs may be placed upon the property for any reason.

Such a restriction would limit the ability of the buyer to place a sign on their property and may be an item of note on the title report.

Any matter that becomes a defect, restriction or other matter against the property must be addressed either prior to close or at closing so that all parties understand what the transfer of the property entails. Specific inclusions that you may encounter are explained more fully within the section pertaining to deeds. You should review these chapters carefully to be sure that you are able to explain any inclusions or exclusions that may be applicable to a property for which you are conducting the closing.

TITLE COMMITMENT AND INSURANCE

At times, the title commitment and insurance issuance will be conducted with the individuals outside of closing. At other times, you will present these documents at the closing table. It is important that you understand the form and inclusions of such documents prior to presenting them.

Title insurance is the guarantee of what the buyer is receiving when they purchase a piece of real property. The title insurance policy will provide the borrower with the details of the title to the property they are purchasing as it appears in public records. From the search, the title insurance company agrees to defend against any defects that might arise.

In other words, the obtainment of insurance provides the buyer with the assurance that if any item was missed during the search process, the buyer will not be responsible for any costs that might arise in the future in relationship to this lack of knowledge.

A variety of potential defects might become known in the future. For example,

- a deed could contain a clerical error

- incorrect marital status might have been entered on a deed of conveyance

- undisclosed heirs in a past property transfer might come forth to claim interest in the property in the future

- the signature on deed transfer documentation by any individual deemed unable to sign such documents like a minor or an incompetent individual

These are not the only instances in which title insurance may become important but are a few examples so that you will have a better understanding of why title insurance might prove beneficial to an individual buyer even when the title search indicated no defects within the chain of title. Each of these instances defines a situation where the abstractor researching the title would not have knowledge of a potential defect that could affect the ownership interest of the new buyer of a piece of real estate.

Title insurance remains in effect until the interest that is being insured is transferred. In other words, coverage will remain in effect until the property is transferred to another party. At the next transfer of the property, another title search will be conducted and new insurance will be issued to the new owners. The lender or the buyer may purchase title insurance coverage to protect their interest.

CHAPTER

8

DEEDS

As a settlement agent, you must gain a fundamental knowledge of the inclusions, exclusions, limitations and restrictions that may be incorporated into the deed or implied by the deed form used as the transfer instrument. Each type of deed carries specific implications as to the status of the title, the rights to the property being conveyed, the warranties and covenants of the seller and the estate and interest being granted to the buyer. Each transaction you close will use a deed to convey or transfer the interest from the seller to the buyer. You should ensure that you have a solid knowledge base regarding the variety of deeds you will encounter during your settlement functions.

A property may be transferred by a variety of deed types. Each type of deed carries different warranties.

Deeds convey or transfer the ownership interest in land from one person or entity to another.

Conveyance may be either voluntary or involuntary.

A deed of conveyance is defined as a written instrument that is executed and delivered by an owner of real property for the purpose of transferring title or interest in the property to another individual or entity.

GENERAL WARRANTY DEED

A general warranty deed is considered the best deed a buyer can receive. General warranty deeds often contain all of the covenants and warranties listed later in this section. This type of deed is used most extensively across the United States.

This deed states that the Grantor (seller) warrants good, clear title to the grantee (buyer) and agrees to protect the grantee from any defect in the title whether the defect occurred during the seller's ownership or that of previous owners.

In other words, the seller is guaranteeing that the title is clear and that they will defend the position of the buyer if some matter appears at some point in the future that might limit the buyer's interest.

This is the most common deed you will encounter in your closing functions and is among the most easily insured deeds from the perspective of the title insurance company.

GRANT DEED

Some states regularly use a grant deed. In a grant deed, the seller warrants only the time of his possession of the title.

These coverings are fewer in number and narrower in coverage than those found in the general warranty deed.

This applies especially to the covenant regarding encumbrances.

In a general warranty deed, the grantor makes himself responsible for the encumbrances of prior owners as well as his own actions.

The grant deed limits the grantor's responsibility to the period of time he actually owned the property.

The primary reason for the development and use of title insurance is the grant deed. Insurance coverage regarding the title gives the buyer protection if a flaw in the title is later discovered.

The grant deed is similar in nature to the special warranty deeds and will sometimes fall under the same terminology.

SPECIAL WARRANTY DEED

In the special warranty deed, the seller warrants the property title only against defect occurring during the seller's ownership and not against defect existing before that time.

Executors and trustees who speak on behalf of an estate often use the special warranty deed. The executor or trustee has no authority to warrant or defend the acts of previous owners of the title. The buyer can protect himself against later discoveries by purchasing title insurance.

The special warranty deed has been known in some states as the bargain and sale deed.

In summary, the grantor warrants good, clear title to the grantee and agrees to protect and defend the grantee from all defects in the title that occurred during the grantor's ownership. In other words, the seller is guaranteeing that he has cleared the title from all defects during his ownership but is making no guarantees as to the condition of the title because of the actions of previous owners.

BARGAIN AND SALE DEED

The basic bargain sale deed contains no covenants and only the minimal essentials of the deed. The deed

- Identifies the buyer in the seller

- Recites consideration

- Describes the property

- Contains words of conveyance

- Contains the seller signature

The deed has no covenants, and in this deed, the seller only implies that he owns the property described in the deed making no guarantee as to any condition of the title including the right to transfer the property.

In most cases, a buyer acquiring a bargain and sale deed will desire a full abstract or title search and the title insurance policy

The grantor implies that he owns an interest in the property but conveys the property without any warranty to the grantee.

In this case, it would be most prudent to have a professional title search performed. These deeds are often used for the quick transfer of real estate and carry no guarantees as to the condition of the title.

QUITCLAIM DEED

A quitclaim deed has no covenants or warranties whatsoever.

- The grantor makes no statement nor is it even implied that he owns the property.

- Whatever rights the seller possesses at the time the deed is delivered are conveyed to the buyer.

- If the seller has no interest or title to the property described in the deed no interest is conveyed to the buyer.

- If the seller possesses fee simple title, the fee simple title will be conveyed to the buyer.

The critical wording in a quitclaim deed is the seller's statement that he does remise, relief and quitclaim forever.

- o Quitclaim actually means to renounce all possession or interest.

- o Remise means to give up any existing claim.

If the grantor of a quitclaim deed subsequently acquires any other interest in the property, he is not required to convey it to the buyer.

Initially it may seem that this type of deed has no effective use. However, situations often arise in transactions when a person claimed to have a partial ownership interest in a parcel of land.

Example: An ownership interest is discovered as a title defect or cloud of the title.

This defective interest may result from an inheritance, community property or mortgage foreclosure sale as well as from other means.

By releasing any claim to the fee simple with a quitclaim deed, the cloud on the fee owner's title is removed.

- The quitclaim deed can be used to create easements as well as relief of easements.

- The quitclaim deed can be used to release remainder and reversion interests.

- The quitclaim deed can be used to remove the interest of a party in a creative financing scenario.

- Some buyers who default on the payment of their mortgage may choose to enact a quitclaim deed rather than endure a foreclosure proceeding.

In a quitclaim deed, the Grantor coveys whatever interests or claims they have in a property without any warranty or the implication that they own a portion of the property.

These deeds are frequently used in an effort to clear title blemishes of perceived claims when a property is being transferred. It may occur that a closing you are conducting requires the completion of a quitclaim deed from a third party before the transaction can be finalized. You should become familiar with the inclusions and purposes of a quitclaim deed so that you can provide a general explanation to the parties of your transaction in the event a quitclaim deed becomes a part of the closing process.

GIFT DEED   A gift deed is created when the phrase for money or other valuable consideration is replaced with the statement in consideration of his or her natural love and affection or a similar statement.

This phrase may be used in a general warranty, special warranty, or grant deed however; it is most often used in a quitclaim or bargain sale deed.

GUARDIAN'S
DEED

A guardian's deed is used to convey a minor's interest in a property.

This deed must contain the information that the legal authority usually, the court order, permits the guardians convey a minors property.

SHERRIFF'S DEED/
REFEREE'S DEED

These deeds are issued to the new buyer when a person's real estate is sold because of a mortgage or other court ordered foreclosure sale.

This type of deed conveys only the foreclosed party's title and carries only one covenant.

This covenant states that the sheriff or referee has not damaged the property title.

DEED IN LIEU OF
FORECLOSURE

A deed in lieu of foreclosure may be created in an effort to avoid the full foreclosure action.

The debtor conveys to the lender the property, including any equity, in consideration of the removal of all obligations to pay the debt on the part of the debtor.

A deed in lieu of foreclosure may only be executed after the default on the part of the debtor.

CORRECTION
DEED

A correction deed or deed of confirmation is used to correct an error in a previously executed and delivered deed.

Example: A correction deed is created because an error was found in the spelling of the names or property description on a previous deed.

A quitclaim deed is often used to the same purpose.

A correction deed may also be called a deed of confirmation or a reformation deed.

The use of this type of deed is extremely limited. This type of deed may only be used if an item to be corrected is:

- Clerical or Typographical

- To cure a lack of clarifying information

- To cure a defective acknowledgement

CESSION DEED   A cession deed is a form of quitclaim deed where a property owner conveys certain rights to the county or municipality.

INTER-SPOUSAL DEED   An inter-spousal deed is used in some states to transfer real property between spouses.

TAX DEED   A tax deed is used to conveyed title to real estate that has been sold by the government because of the nonpayment of taxes.

DEED OF TRUST   A deed of trust may be used to convey real estate to a third party as security for a loan.

These are not all of the conceivable forms of deeds you may encounter in your closing functions. These are simply the most commonly used and accepted deeds. The sample on the following pages will detail a full warranty deed. Many of the other deeds you will encounter will contain less information than the full warranty deed.

You should review the form and inclusions in any deed that relates to a closing you conduct. If any item exists that you do not understand, you should gain the necessary explanations prior to conducting the closing.

You should also confirm that they form of the deed provided to you for the closing matches the expected or negotiated form from the sales contract.

Any alteration to the form of the deed can affect the buyer's interest in the property as described above and may be an issue that needs addressed prior to finalizing the transfer of the property.

KENNEY

Parcel ID No.

File No.

This Indenture, made the _____ day of _____, 20 _____

Between

(hereinafter called Grantor) of the one part and

(hereinafter called Grantee) of the other part.

    Witnesseth, that the said Grantor for and in consideration of
_____ dollars ($_____) lawful
money of the United States of America, unto him well and truly paid by the
said Grantee, at or before the sealing and delivery hereof, the receipt whereof
is hereby acknowledged, has granted, bargained, and sold, released, and
confirmed, and by these presents does grant, bargain and sell, release and
confirm unto the said Grantee, as the sole owner.

All that certain lot or piece of ground situate in _____
_____ being lot No ____,
Page _____ being more fully described as follows

    Bounded on the northwest by Pine street, on the Southwest by lot No.
200-17-21B (now or formerly of Mr. Jones et al); fronting twenty-five (25)
feet on the Southeast side of First Avenue, between 3rd and 4th Streets and
extending back at an equal width to a depth of One Hundred Twenty (120)
feet.

    Being known and numbered as Premises 322 First Avenue.

    Being further identified as This County Tax Parcel Number 200-17-
19A

    Also ALL those certain lots or pieces of ground situate in This County
in the City of Nod, County of There, and State of Freedom.

Figure 8:1 Sample General Warranty Deed Page 1

Together with all and singular the buildings and improvements, ways, streets, alleys, driveways, passages, waters, water-courses, rights, liberties, privileges, hereditaments, and appurtenances whatsoever unto the hereby granted premises belonging or in anywise appertaining, and the revisions and remainders, rents, issues, and profits thereof; and all the estate, right, title, interest, property, claim and demand whatsoever of him, the said grantor, as well at the laws in equity, of, in and to the same.

To have and to hold the said lot or piece of ground described above, with the buildings and improvements thereon erected, hereditaments and premises hereby granted, or mentioned and intended so to be, with the appurtenances, unto the said Grantee, here heirs and assigns, to and for the only property use and behoof of the said Grantee, her heirs and assigns, forever.

And the said Grantor, for herself and her heirs, executors and administrators, does, by these presents, covenant, grant and agree, to and with the said Grantee, her heirs and assigns, that he, the said Grantor, and his heirs, and against all and every other person and persons whosoever lawfully claiming or to claim the same or any part thereof, by, from or under him, her, it, or any of them shall and will.

Warrant and Forever Defend

In Witness Whereof, the party of the first part has hereunto set his hand and seal. Dated the day and year first above written.

Sealed and Delivered
IN THE PRESENCE OF US:

{Seal

Figure 8:2 Sample Form – Deed Page 2

This form is included for example purposes only. The form is modified from the acceptable real estate forms as released by HUD. The services of a real estate professional should be retained to ensure the correct forms are used for your transaction

FORM   The deed must take the form required by statutory law if any exists.

NAMES   The names of the parties, both the buyer(s) and the seller(s), must be included on the deed.

- This section should be fully completed and concise.

- The exact names as detailed on the sales agreement should be used for the parties named.

- Marital status of each party should be detailed.

- Any name changes should be included in this portion of the deed.

- Name changes can be noted as *"formerly known as..."*.

CAPACITY   The parties to the deed must have legal capacity to enter a binding agreement as defined by statute.

CONSIDERATION   A statement that the property is being sold for payment of either good or valuable consideration must be included.

- This is the purchase price of the property.

In some states, you may maintain the privacy of the transfer by inserting a nominal amount of money plus other consideration with a phrase such as *"$1.00 plus other good and valuable consideration"*.

Consideration may also take the form of a gift.

GRANTING CLAUSE   This states what act the parties are performing. In other words, this clause signifies the intent of the seller to convey the property to the buyer.

LEGAL DESCRIPTION   This is a very exact description of the property, not the physical address.

The exact description is the legal description that does not depend on potentially altering addresses.

The legal description allows one to locate and identify the property to be conveyed and distinguishes the property from all other real estate.

RECITAL

This identifies previous owners from whom the current grantor took title. It aids in obtaining a chain of title by reciting backwards from this transaction to allow a searcher to find the next piece in the chain in reverse.

REALTY TAX STAMPS

These are obtained at the courthouse of record and are essential to the recordation of the deed. These provide proof that the state and local taxes to transfer real property have been paid.

TO HAVE AND TO HOLD CLAUSE

This is also known as the habendum and is the technical language that describes the ownership that is being transferred.

GRANTOR'S SIGNATURE The grantors (sellers) are the parties who must sign the deed.

No signature of acceptance by the grantee (buyer) must be included to affect a legal transfer.

ACKNOWLEDGEMENT This is best known as notarizing.

This is the event where the sellers appear before you or another approved person to prove and declare that the signing of the deed and the transfer of the deed is a voluntary act.

CERTIFICATE OF GRANTEE'S ADDRESS

This is another requirement that must be met in order to record the deed.

This provides the new owner information that allows the taxing authorities to send all future notices and tax bills to the grantee.

RECORDING REFERENCE

This is typically included by the clerk of record and specifies the date, deed-book volume and deed-book page number where the recorded document is filed.

DELIVERY AND ACCEPTANCE

While there is no requirement that the grantees sign the deed document, the last legal step in the transfer of the deed is the delivery and acceptance of the conveyance.

The grantee must receive and accept the document.

This acceptance finalizes the transaction and conveyance of the property has been achieved.

Delivery may be actual or constructive.

ACTUAL DELIVERY is the physical transfer of the deed before the death of the grantor.

CONSTRUCTIVE DELIVERY is the delivery in cases where the law implies the existence of delivery by the conduct of the parties involved.

WARRANTIES OF TITLE

A deed meeting all the requirements detailed could still leave some important questions unanswered. These are questions pertaining to the grantors right to transfer title and the exact interest in the property being conveyed by the deed.

The grantee will often ask grantor to include certain covenants and warranties in the deed.

These are written promises by the grantors regarding the condition of the title.

Five different covenants have evolved over the centuries for use in deeds.

The deed may contain none, some or all of these covenants and warranties. There may be additional warranties that exist within the jurisdiction in which you conduct your closings.

COVENANT OF SEIZIN Under the covenant a seizin, the grantor guarantees that he is the owner and possessor of the property being conveyed and that they actually have the right to convey the property.

If a matter comes to light that shows another individual held an interest in the property that was not removed or if the seller did not hold total interest, the seller agrees to defend the rights of the buyer in court or financially.

COVENANT OF ENJOYMENT

Under the covenant of enjoyment, the seller warranties or guaranties that someone else who claims an interest in the property will not disturb the buyer.

Similar to the covenant of seizin, the seller is stating that they will take the actions required to cure any interest or claim of interest that another party brings against the new property owner.

COVENANT AGAINST ENCUMBRANCES

The covenants against encumbrances is when the seller guarantees to the buyer that the title is not encumbered with any easements, restrictions, unpaid property taxes, assessments, mortgages, judgments, etc. except as stated in the deed.

If the buyer discovers an undisclosed encumbrance, he can sue the seller for the cost of removing it.

COVENANT OF FURTHER ASSURANCE

The covenant of further assurance requires the seller to procure and deliver to the buyer any subsequent documents that might be necessary to make good the buyer's title.

WARRANTY DEED FOREVER

Warranty deed forever is the guarantee to the buyer that the seller will bear the expense of defending the buyer's title.

If at any time in future, someone else attempts to and is able to prove that he is the rightful owner of the property, the seller will bear the burden of the costs incurred. The buyer can sue the seller for damages up to the value the property.

COVENANT OF RIGHT TO CONVEY

The covenant of right to convey is an assurance that the grantor has the right to convey the property. In some jurisdictions, this warranty is covered under the covenant of seizin.

**COVENANT OF
NON-CLAIM**   The convent of non-claim assures the grantee that neither the grantor nor his heirs or assigns will claim any title to the property being conveyed.

The more covenants and warranties the seller includes in the deed of conveyance the more solid the transfer can be considered.

Because the warranties are tremendous, promises on the part of the seller, the seller will often desire title insurance to back up the warranty being made.

The buyer can feel more comfortable if the deed is backed up by title insurance because they know any costs incurred in the future will be covered and that the title has been properly researched.

LIMITATIONS IN THE DEED

At times, the deed may contain limitations regarding the rights and interests being transferred to the buyer or the actions the buyer may take in the future regarding the piece of property. These limitations can vary depending on the specific situation and the exact wording of the deed to the transaction. Limitations typically take one of three forms.

Exceptions   Exceptions withhold or exclude a part of the estate or land being conveyed from transfer or conveyance. They represent specific property rights that are not being conveyed as part of the transfer.

Example: A common exception would be if the grantor required the use of an easement across a portion of his property that is being sold or conveyed in order to continue to access another portion of his property that he is retaining.

An exception of this type would be shown as an exception Schedule B of the title commitment. When you locate an exception within the deed or title commitment, you should confirm that this exception is understood by all parties to the transaction prior to continuing with the closing.

Reservations   Reservations are clauses that reserve an interest in the title being conveyed. Reservations are created in the favor of the grantor.

Example: A common reservation would be a reservation regarding mineral rights. The seller may wish to retain the mineral rights or may have transferred the rights to another party in a different transaction.

These reservations would be shown as an exception Schedule B of the title commitment and might appear in the deed. When you locate a reservation within deed or title commitment, you should confirm that this exception is understood by all parties to the transaction prior to continuing with the closing.

Restriction   Restrictions may be incorporated into the deed. A restriction is a limitation on the future action a buyer may take with the property.

        Example: A common restriction would be to limit new construction on the property to buildings of less than 15 feet in height. This restriction would protect the scenic views of other property owners in the area.

        These restrictions would be shown as an exception Schedule B of the title commitment and may appear on the deed. When you locate a restriction within the deed or title commitment, you should confirm that this exception is understood by all parties to the transaction prior to continuing with the closing.

The actual form of the deeds you will review will vary. Each State and Jurisdiction will have variations within the form of the deeds you will see. Deed form has altered through the years causing still more variety. Providing all of the legal components exist within the document, any individual may create their own deed without seeking the aid or advice of a legal professional. We have included an example of a deed on the preceding pages to assist you in gaining an overview of the placement and general format of the deeds you will encounter. It is important that you review each deed you encounter to ensure that you comprehend all of the possible warranties, covenants, restrictions, exceptions or reservations prior to the closing.

The deed that we have shown provides you with the form of a fully executed general warranty deed. You may encounter other deed forms during your settlement duties. Other common deed forms you will encounter include the bargain and sale, sheriff's deed and tax deed. The following pages provide an illustration of a sample tax deed that will enable you to compare the inclusions and exclusions of each document. You should note that the legally binding components of the deed are the same but the wording, warranties and covenants vary dramatically from one deed form to the next.

Parcel ID No.

File No.

JUDIICAL SALE IN CONNECTION WITH THE TAX SALE OF 20___

DEED

OF

TAX CLAIM BUREAU OF ANY COUNTY, ANYWHERE

Made the _____ day of _____, Two Thousand _____ (20___)

Between the TAX CLAIM BUREAU OF _____ COUNTY (the latter a subdivision of the City of _____ with a seat of government in the Borough of _____ County of _____ and Commonwealth of _____) as constituted and created by virtue of the provisions of the Act of Assembly approved the 7th day of July, 1947, P.L. 1368 (72 PS 5860.101) and known as the "Real Estate Tax Sale Law" as supplemented and amended, as trustee for

Owner or reputed owners, herein designated as Grantor of Party of the First Part;

AND

of the City of _____, County of _____, and Commonwealth or State of _____, herein designated as Grantee or Party of the Second Part;

Witnesseth THAT WHEREAS, the real estate hereinafter identified was exposed to the Tax Sale duly held by the First Party on the _____ day of _____, 20 ___, as continued, adjourned, or readjourned, under and by virtue of the provisions of the Act of Assembly hereinbefore identified and the upset price was not bid by anyone is such Sale; and

WITNESSETH, THAT WHEREAS, by proceedings filed to No. _____ a Decree of the Court of Common Please of _____ County, was entered directing that said property be sold at a subsequent date fixed by the Court, free and clear of all tax and municipal claims, mortgages, liens, charges, and estates, of whatsoever kind, with the purchaser at said sale to have an absolute title to said property, free and clear of the claims aforesaid;

AND WHEREAS, the Second Party became the purchaser, (or is the heir or assignee of said purchaser) of said real estate at the Judicial Sale held by the First Party on the _____ day of _____ A.D. 20 ___, as continued, adjourned, or readjourned, under and by virtue of the provisions of the Act of Assembly hereinbefore identified.

NOW, THEREFORE, WITNESSETH, that under and in pursuance of the Act of Assembly aforesaid and the Order of Court entered in connection, therewith, and for and in consideration of $_____ _____ Dollars, in hand paid, the receipt of which is herewith acknowledged, (being the price bid at said Judicial Sale), the receipt of which is herewith acknowledged, (being the price bid at said Judicial Sale), the Grantor or Party of the First Part, under and by virtue of the Act of Assembly aforesaid as Trustee for the owner or reputed owner of said Real

Figure 7:3 Sample Form – Tax Deed Page 1

REAL ESTATE CLOSING - SETTLEMENT AGENT

Estate, does hereby grant, bargain, sell, assign, and release, in fee simple, unto the said Grantee or Party of the Second Part, their heirs, successors, and assigns,

ALL

Control # 060-0027

Map # 0800-21-17B

For chain of title see DBV 1128 page 116

All taxes up to and including 20____ County and Township were in sale.

Realty transfer tax is $_____ for 1% Local and $_____ for 1% State, based on the Common Level Ratio Factor at the time of the sale, which was 11.91%.

TO the end that said purchaser shall take and hold an absolute title to the said property free and clear of all tax and municipal claims, mortgages, liens, charges, and estates of whatsoever kind, except ground rent separately taxed.

TO HAVE AND TO HOLD the said premises, without warranty of any kind or nature, unto the said Party of the Second Part, their heirs, successors, and assigns forever.

IN WITNESS WHEREOF, the said Party of the First Part set its hand and seal the day and year aforesaid.

Figure 7:4 Sample Tax Deed Page 2

Recorder's Use Only

QUITCLAIM DEED

FOR A VALUABLE CONDIERATION.   HEREBY QUITCLAIM to:

The real property in the County of _____, State of _____ described as

Witness my hand this _____ day of _____, 20 ____.

_____   _____

State of   }   Witness my hand and official seal:
                                            }
County of   }
On _____, 20___   _____
Before me, the undersigned, a Notary Public   Notary Public in and for Said County and State
and for said County and State personally
appeared   NOTARY SEAL

Proved to me on the basis of satisfactory evidence to be the
person whose name is (are) sub-scribed to the instrument and
acknowledge that

executed the same.

Figure 7:5 Sample Quit Claim Deed

HOW TITLE IS HELD AND TRANSFERRED

A portion of your function at the closing table will be to verify the identity of all individuals signing paperwork in relationship to the transaction. This will typically be accomplished by the review and obtainment of a copy of a valid driver's license indicating the names and applicable information of the individuals who will sign. In addition to the verification of the identity of the individuals signing documents, you must make certain that the documents are signed by all of the applicable parties.

D uring the search and document preparation processes, information will be verified so that all known parties in a transaction will be present for the signing. The documents provided to you for the actual closing will contain the full names of the individuals who will sign.

You must verify that the signatures are created exactly as they appear on the documents.

Example: A specific document could be created using the names

Mary Smith

Mary J. Smith

Mary Jane Smith

and all indicate the same individual.

You should verify that the signature form matches the typewritten form of the name on each document signed.

In relationship to the signing of documents, you should gain an understanding of the types of ownership that may be transferred.

There are varieties of ownership forms in existence and any owner may have created issues that must be carefully reviewed so that you can ensure that the proper individuals have signed all of the documents. Improper endorsement on a closing document may create an issue later that may become a defect on the title or, at times, invalidate the closing you are conducting.

Sole Ownership   Sole ownership is also known as Tenancy by Severalty. This means the ownership is cut off from other owners or the individual owns the property alone.

In Sole Ownership, the term individual may refer to a variety of entities. Ownership must be a single entity but can include:

Married or single individuals

Corporations considered a single entity

This form of ownership is both created and disposed of by deed or will.

When a sole owner holds the title to the property you are closing, the individual must sign the transaction documents.

Concurrent Ownership   Ownership may also be concurrent ownership. Concurrent ownership is the ownership of a property by two or more individuals.

These owners can share one of five different unites.

- **Unity of Time** They may have the Unity of Time, which means that both parties acquired their interest at the same instant in time.

- **Unity of Title** They may share the Unity of Title, which means that their interest was acquired by the same instrument.

- **Unity of Possession**

  They may share the Unity of Possession. This means that each party has the same, undivided right to possess or use the property. In the Unity of Possession, all portions are owned equally.

- **Unity of Interest**

  They may share the Unity of Interest. The Unity of Interest means that each owner has an equal interest regardless of the amount they contribute or their desire to have different interests.

- **Unity of Person**

  They may share the Unity of Person, which means that each owner owns the property as a unity or team. An example of this would be a married couple forming one legal unit in the process of ownership.

Concurrent ownership may take many forms. These forms are referred to as a type of tenancy. Each tenancy will carry different rights that will affect the individuals who must sign the transfer documents.

- Joint Tenancy

- Tenancy in common

- Community Property

- Sole Proprietorship

Each of these methods of holding title carries different ramifications including the ability to transfer ownership, to assign interest to heirs and assigns and tax consequences. It is important for you to understand the different types of ownership because each type will require a different set of signatures to either transfer or take ownership of the property you are closing.

TYPE OF OWNERSHIP	NUMBER OR INDIVIDUALS	AMOUNT OF INTEREST	SIGNATURES FOR SALE
Joint Tenancy	Two or more people	Equal interest according to contract	Each individual owner may sell their interest without the consent of the other parties. All parties must sign for a full transfer of ownership.
Tenancy in Common	Two or more people	Equal or unequal interest	Each individual owner may sell their interest without the consent of the other parties.
Community Property / Tenancy by the entirety	Ownership between spouses only	Equal interest	The property may only be sold with the partners consent and both signatures are required.
Sole Ownership	One Person	Undivided / sole interest	Only the single owner's signature is required.

These are not the only methods of holding title, only a detail of the most common that you will encounter. If you are closing a loan that contains ownership with which you are unfamiliar, contact the company or individual who prepared the search and the documents that you are witnessing to determine the alterations to standard procedures you must make to close the transaction competently.

AGREEMENT TO CHANGE TITLE FROM JOINT TENANCY TO COMMUNITY PROPERTY

1. PARTIES:

Parties to this agreement are _____

and _____.

2. RECITALS:

a) The parties hereto are husband and wife, residing in the County of _____ State of _____.

b) They have heretofore held property in their common or separate names, and may hereafter do so.

c) They hold portions of their property in joint tenancy only as a matter of convenience or transfer.

d) This agreement is entered into with the full knowledge on the part of each party of the extent and probable value of all of the property and estate of the community, and of the separate and joint property of each other, ownership of which would be conferred by law on each of them in the event of the termination of their relationship by death or otherwise.

e) It is the express intent of the parties hereto that all their common properties are and shall be their community property.

3. AGREEMENT THAT ALL PROPERTY SHALL BE COMMUNITY

Each party hereby releases all of his or her separate rights in and to any and all property, real or personal and wherever situated, which either party now owns or has an interest in, and each party agrees that all property or interest therein owned heretofore or presently or hereafter acquired by either from common funds shall be deemed to be community property of the parties hereto, whether held in their separate names, as joint tenants, as tenants in common, or in any other legal form. The parties understand that this agreement will automatically, without other formality, transfer to the other a one-half interest in any separate property now owned and that such transfer could constitute a taxable gift under Federal and State law.

4. AGREEMENT MODIFIABLE IN WRITING ONLY:

This agreement shall not be modified except in writing signed by both parties, or by the mutual written surrender or abandonment of their said community interest in accordance with the laws of said State pertaining to the management of community property, or by the termination of their marriage by death or otherwise.

Dated:_____ 20 _____

_____   _____

Figure 9:2 Sample Tenancy Change Form

CHAPTER

10

LOAN COMMITMENT AND SECURITY INSTRUMENTS

Many of the transactions for which you will conduct a closing will contain a mortgage loan that assists the buyer in gaining the funds necessary for the purchase. The sales contract will often contain clauses pertaining to the application, approval and terms of a mortgage loan. When the application and approval timelines have been met by the buyer, the terms of the loan program approval become important to the final closing documents.

Each component of the loan commitment and instructions will effect the settlement and the processes, documents and transaction specifics that you will follow. Most of your closing specifics will come from the Sales Agreement and the Lender Instructions. The completion of the loan package documents will become a critical function for you at the closing table. You should review each of the following documents carefully to confirm that you understand the inclusions and implications contained within each one that you may encounter at the closing table.

The following pages are examples of actual closing instructions for a purchase loan. Following each instruction page, the applicable documents are included for your review. You should scrutinize each document and the applicable explanatory training entries to confirm that you understand the inclusions since these documents will make up a large portion of your function as a settlement agent. It is important to note that as the settlement agent, you should not offer legal advice to the individuals involved in the closing. While you should gain a familiarity with the closing documents you will witness, you should direct any questions pertaining to the inclusions and specifics to the individual or company that generated the documents. For instance, the inclusions and specifics of the note and mortgage documents should be addressed by the Mortgage Lender, Loan Processor or Closing Team at the Lending Institution that handled the loan package.

Loan#	LENDER'S CLOSING INSTRUCTIONS	Date

Borrower

Property Address:

Return Original Signed Documents to Lender:

Loan Terms
Loan Amount:
Interest Rate:
Term
Loan Type:
Loan Purpose:
____ 1st MTG or ____ 2nd MTG
Estimated Funding Date

Settlement Agent

Title Company

Phone:
Fax:
Email:
Attn:
Closing #:

Phone:
Fax:
Email:
Attn:
Order #:

1.   LOAN DISBURSEMENTS

FEE	POC	BUYER	SELLER	LENDER	OTHER	HUD-1 PAYABLE TO
801 Origination Points						
802 Lender Discount Pints						
803 Lender Appraisal Fee to						
804 Lender Credit Report to						
805 Lender Inspection						
806 Mortgage Insurance Ap Fee						
807 Assumption Fee						
808						
809						
810 Administration Fee to						
811 Application Fee to						
812 Processing Fee to						
813 Wire Transfer Fee to						
814 Underwriting Fee to						
815 Flood Cert to						
816 Tax Service to						
817 Buydown Fee to						
818						
819						
820						
821						
901 Prepaid Int (days @ /day)						
902 PMI Premium						
903 Property Insurance						
904 Flood Insurance						
905 VA Funding Fee						
906						
1001 Property Ins (pmts @ /mth)						
1002 Mortgage Ins (pmts @ /mth)						

10:1 Example – Lender's Closing Instructions

1003 City Taxes (pmts @ /mth)
1004 County Tax (pmts @ /mth)
1005 Annual Asmnt (pmts @ /mth)
1006 Flood Ins (pmts @ /mth)
1007 School Taxes (pmts @ /mth)
1008 (pmts @ /mth)
1009 Aggregate Adjustment
1101 Settlement or Closing Fee
1102 Abstract or Title Search
1103 Title Examination
1104 Title Ins Binder
1105 Document Prep fee
1106 Notary Fee
1107 Attorney's Fee
1108 Title Insurance
1111
1112
1113
1201 Recording Fees
1202 City Taxes & Stamps
1203 State Taxes & Stamps
1204
1205
1301 Survey
1302 Pest Inspection
1303 Final Inspection to
1304
1305 Review Appraiser to
703 Commission Paid At Settlement
Totals

   a)   Other than the fees listed, no other fees or charges may be charged without prior approval from Lender.
   b)   Additional compensation of $ will be paid by Lender to   . This amount is not deducted from the principal balance of the loan. The compensation must show on HUD-1 as "Broker Fee paid by Lender POC"
   c)   Unless notified otherwise by Lender, we will remit our wire to you in the amount of the loan, less fees paid to Lender. The "Broker Fee paid by Lender POC" will be included in the wire when applicable.

2.   PAYOFFS   COMPANY   ACCOUNT #   AMT. TO BE PAID

3.   REQUIREMENTS: The documents or requirements indicated below must be executed or satisfied. You are responsible to ensure that each borrower receives two signed, dated and fully completed copies of the NOTICE OF RIGHT TO CANCEL (if applicable) and one copy of the FEDERAL TRUTH-IN-LENDING DISCLOSURE STATEMENT.

__ Deed/Mortgage with applicable riders	__ Note with Applicable Addendums
__ Federal Truth-In-Lending Disclosure Statement	__ Original Application to be signed
__ Power of attorney (original)	__ Request for taxpayer's ID (IRS W-9)
__ Right to cancel notice	__ Typed application to be signed
__ Certified proof of funds to close	__ Itemization of amount financed
__ Tax Certification form	__ Grant/Warranty Deed
__	
__	

4.   FUNDING CONDITIONS: The following approval conditions remain outstanding. Borrower is being allowed to sign documents subject to Lender's receipt and approval of these conditions. You are not authorized to disburse funds until Lender has approved the following:
    HUD to be faxed to   for review and approval
    Need certified copy of warranty deed (for CA grant deed) signed by seller(s)
    Need copy of certified funds buyer bring for closing costs (CAN'T DISBURSE FUNDS WITHOUT IT)
    Need evidence of hazard insurance, paid for one year
    All taxes to be current at close
    All signed docs to be returned to us immediately after signing in return fed-ex envelope provided

5.   In connection with this loan, we enclose the necessary documents requiring signature and acknowledgement where applicable. All loan documents must be executed exactly as the names are shown below the signature lines. No alterations or erasures to these documents are permitted without our approval.

10:1 Example – Lender's Closing Instructions

    a. A Specific Power of Attorney cannot execute documents, without prior approval from Lender. A General Power of Attorney will not be accepted. Examples of POA signatures

        John Jones by Nancy Jones as Attorney in fact. Initials should read as JJ by NJ as A.I.F.

        Nancy Jones as Attorney in fact for John Jones. Initials should read NJ as A.I.F. for JJ

6. In addition to the above, return the following:

    b. Original HUD-1 settlement statement with all payees as shown on these instructions. Sellers closing cost credits are limited to non-recurring costs only, and are further limited to 6% (3% for TX home equity) of sales price of the home. Credit can't exceed the actual non-recurring costs. Examples of recurring closing costs are: odd days interest, hazard, flood, windstorm insurance premiums, property taxes, HOA dues. Broker credits must also be included in this 6% credit figure.

    c. Certified copy of all checks for balance due at closing from borrower. Must be certified check, no cash deposits allowed unless approved by lender.

    d. 2 Certified copies of signed, notarized Deed of Trust/Mortgage and Riders

    e. Certified copy of second Deed of Trust/Mortgage and Note in the amount of $, interest rate   %, monthly payment $ and term of

    f. Certified copy of any Grant/Warranty Deed from seller (seller to match Preliminary Title Report), inter-spousal transfer deeds or other quitclaims being executed for this transaction.

    g. Original copy of any and all duly executed Settlement Closing Instructions and amendments thereto, including correct lender, rate and terms.

    h. Copy of borrower's valid photo identification used at closing.

7. We require a standard ALTA Policy within 15 days from the funding of this loan.
SHORT FORM POLICES ARE NOT ALLOWED
Individual title reports required for first and second mortgages. The ALTA Policy must contain a Plat Map or survey Endorsements 100 and Form 8.1 as required without deletion, 116, 115, 116.2 (if subject property is a Condominium Estate), 115.2 (if the subject property is a Planned Unit Development), and Special Endorsements:
With liability in the amount of our loan(s) on the subject property, subject only to:

    a) General and special taxes and assessments not yet due (all such taxes and assessments, which are due as of the settlement date must be paid current at closing) and

    b) Items   as shown on the preliminary report of title No.   date

8. Secondary financing in the amount of $ (none if left blank) has been approved. The total consideration in this transaction except for our loan(s) proceeds and any permitted secondary financing, must be paid in cash. Do not record or disburse funds if you have knowledge or reason to suspect the borrower intends to obtain secondary financing to purchase the subject property other than as permitted herein.

Additionally, you are instructed not to record or disburse funds if you have knowledge or reason to suspect that the purchase price of the subject property is not $ or that any portion of the purchase price is being paid other than with certified funds without prior written authorization from us. No other subordinate financing is allowed without prior written approval from Lender.

9. It is strictly forbidden to allow a Broker, or Broker affiliate company to close our transaction.

10. All closing documents should be executed in BLUE INK.

11. If State requirements exist, a Non borrower must execute a Deed of Trust/Mortgage, Riders, Federal Truth-In-Lending Disclosure Statement, Itemization of Amount Financed, Notice of Right to Cancel, Warranty and Compliance Agreement, Signature Affidavit and AKA Statement, and Correction Agreement Limited Power of Attorney. A valid photo I.D. must also be provided.

12. ALL TRANSACTIONS: Prior to the disbursement of any funds the closing agent must fax to the Lender the documents listed below for their review and approval. Owner occupied refinance transactions may not be disbursed prior to the day following the Rescission expiration date provided to the borrowers on the notice of right to cancel.

        Signature page of: Note and Addendums, Deed of Trust/Mortgage and Riders
        Executed Grant/Warranty Deed witnessed and notarized, if applicable
        Copy of any certified check(s) for funds to close. Remitter must be the borrower's name and drawn on the borrower's bank
        Any specific closing conditions outlined above under FUNDING CONDITIONS
        Executed final HUD-1 statement
        Federal Truth-in-Lending Statement
        Notice of Right to Cancel, if applicable
        Power of Attorney, if applicable

13. We reserve the right to withdraw these instructions and enclosures if this loan is not closed on or before
if for any reason this loan does not close, return all documents, together with these instructions, to the Lender and notify Lender immediately. We will incur no expense in the closing of this transaction unless otherwise noted in these instructions.

10:1 Example – Lender's Closing Instructions

NOTE

A promissory note is a contract between the borrower and the lender. In the case of seller financing, the lender is actually the seller. Often simply referred to as a note, the document must contain certain key components to ensure it is legally binding and enforceable.

- The note must be in writing.

- The note must be between a borrower and a lender both of whom have the ability to enter into a legally binding contract.

- The note will state the borrowers promise to pay a certain sum of money and the terms under which those monies will be paid.

The borrower will sign the note document and the completed note is given to the lender. At times, the completed note will be recorded prior to remitting it to the lender. If recording is a portion of your settlement function, you should review the lender instructions carefully to determine exactly which documents must be recorded.

Promissory notes need not be complicated but they must clearly outline the terms under which the loan is being granted. Terms could include:

- the principal amount of the mortgage

- the interest rate agreed upon

- the date payment is due

- the late charge, if any, incurred when a payment is paid beyond the due date

- the date that these late charges are assessed

- the length of time payments shall be made

- how the payments will be credited on the account

    Example: Payments will credit to interest and then to the principal

- any other details which have been negotiated between the buyer and the seller with regards to the repayment of the agreed to monies

Simply put a promissory note is the written promise to repay a debt and the outlining of the acceptable terms and method for payment.

A promissory note can be obtained from a variety of sources and the notes that you will review at the closings that you oversee may not appear the same as the note included for your review. Notes may contain a variety of contingencies based upon the agreed upon financing secured. Notes will be customized to suit the transaction being completed and as each transaction you close will be different, the notes will be different. The basic elements of the notes will be incorporated regardless of the other inclusions. You should familiarize yourself with the essential elements of the note and review the sample note that we have included for display purposes. The sample note is a highly customized note incorporating all of the financial negotiations outlined within the lender instruction display in this program.

The components of a promissory note allow certain rights to be legally enforced on the part of both the buyer and the seller. The promissory note will be custom designed incorporate all of the negotiated transaction specifics. The promissory notes that you will review in relationship to your closing will have standard features that are common regardless of transaction specifics. These features will include

- A statement that the document is a promissory note

- The location and the date of the notes signing, in other words the specifics of the settlement meeting.

   As with any contract, the location stated in the contract establishes which state laws govern the execution of the document.

- A statement that the borrower has received something of value and promises to pay the debt as described in the note

- The person who is to make the payments will be detailed

   This signature used to endorse the transaction should appear exactly as this entry is printed.

   It is one of your functions to confirm that that the buyer endorses all legal documents using the exact name form entered on the document

- The company or person who is to receive payments will be clearly identified

- The exact mailing address and/or location for delivery of payments will be shown

- The exact debt amount agreed upon by the note will be detailed

- The interest rate on the debt will be detailed

- The date from which interest will be charged and payments shall begin will be shown

- A specific detail pertaining to the amount of the payments to be made including a breakdown of application of the payments toward principal and interest will be entered

- Any changes to the interest rate, such as ARM requirements will be stated and details explaining such changes will be entered

- The prepayment penalty information will be incorporated

Prepayment of all or part of the loan funds prior to a specified date is sometimes penalized as part of the negotiation process. Prepayment penalty regulations vary by state and if a prepayment penalty is to be imposed on a loan, the applicable laws should be fully researched

- The grace period, if any, which is allowed prior to the addition of a late-charge to the payment will be indicated

- The note will often contain a specific clause that provides the lender with the right to accelerate the loan and demand immediate payment of all interest and principal owed if the borrower misses any individual payments

- The wording of the note will typically cause the borrower to agree to pay any costs incurred by the lender if the borrower falls behind on the agreed to payments

- If the promissory note is tied to a mortgage that secures it making this a mortgage loan, the mortgage details will be entered. Without this reference, the note would be a personal loan.

- A specific location will be available where the borrower will sign the note.

The buyer is sometimes referred to as the note maker.

If two or more persons sign the note, it is common to include a statement in the note that the borrowers are jointly and severally making the note.

> This means that the terms of the note and the obligations created are enforceable on the makers as a group or upon each note maker individually.

REAL ESTATE CLOSING - SETTLEMENT AGENT

You will acknowledge that you have witnessed the signatures of the individual note makers and that they are the individuals named within the note document.

In addition to the basic note, you will sometimes be asked to witness addendums and riders to the note. Addendums will typically elaborate on the specific funding clauses contained within the note. These documents should be signed and witnessed in the same manner as the note. If addendums are to be incorporated into the closing package, the closing instruction sheet will indicate what documents must be signed and the closing package will include the applicable documents.

Examples of the rider attachments indicated by the sample Lenders Closing Instruction form are detailed on the following pages. Again, you should become familiar with the general layout of these documents but direct any buyer questions relating to the inclusions to the Lending Company from which the loan funds will originate.

It is important that you remember that notes are customized to suit the transaction. Each transaction you oversee will vary in specifics and so each note may vary in entries. This variation from the norm will be dependent on the needs of the parties in the transaction.

PREPAYMENT NOTE ADDENDUM

This Prepayment Note Addendum is made this   day of   and is incorporated into and shall be deemed to amend and supplement the Note of the same date (the "Note") given by the undersigned (the "Borrower) to evidence the Borrower's indebtedness to

ADDITIONAL COVENANTS.   Notwithstanding anything to the contrary set forth in the Note or Security Instrument, Borrower and Lender further covenant and agree as follows:

1. Section 5 of the Adjustable Rate Note, is modified to provide for a prepayment charge upon Borrower's full prepayment. A "full prepayment" is the prepayment of all of the unpaid principal due under the Note. A prepayment of only part of the principal is known as a "partial prepayment".

Borrower can make a partial prepayment at anytime without paying nay charge. Borrower may make a full prepayment anytime subject to a prepayment charge as follows:

If within the first   months after the date Borrower executes the Note, Borrower makes a full prepayment (including prepayments occurring as a result of the acceleration of the maturity of the Note), Borrower must, as a condition precedent to a full prepayment, pay a prepayment charge on any amount prepaid in any 12 month period in excess of 20% of the unpaid balance. The prepayment charge will equal the interest that would accrue during a six-month period on the Excess Principal calculated at the rate of interest in effect under the terms of the Note at the time of the full prepayment.

2. All other provisions of the note are unchanged by this addendum and remain in full force and effect.

NOTICE TO BORROWER

Do not sign this loan agreement before you read it. This loan agreement provides for the payment of a penalty if you wish to repay the loan prior to the date provided for repayment in the loan agreement.

Figure 10:4 Sample Prepayment Note Addendum

MAILING ADDRESS CONFIRMATION / PAYMENT LETTER

From:

Re: Loan #   *** IMPORTANT, PLEASE READ THROUGHOULY ***
       Property Address

To:

Dear Homeowner:

A.   All mortgage servicing correspondence will be mailed to the above referenced property address. In order to ensure proper receipt of all mortgage servicing notifications (i.e. monthly statement, Q&A booklets, etc.) please indicate the correct mailing address if it is different from the property address. The address to mail payments and the phone number to call for customer service are listed below.

    Please indicate (X):

    ( )   The property address is correct as referenced above and should be used for correspondence.

    ( )   The proper mailing address is: _____

_____

B.   The monthly payments on the above loan are to begin on _____ , and will continue monthly until

    Your monthly payment will consist of the following:

MONTHLY PAYMENT ....$ _____
MMI/PMI INSRUANCE .... _____
RESERVE FOR COUNTY TAXES .... _____
RESERVE FOR HAXARD INSURANCE................................. _____
RESERVE FOR FLOOD INSURANCE............................... _____
RESERVE FOR CITY TAXES.. _____
RESERVE FOR ANNUAL ASSESSMENT................................ _____
RESERVE FOR SCHOOL TAXES.. _____
_____
          TOTAL MONTHLY PAYMENTS.........$ _____

*** Please be aware that if you have an impound account, you may see a change in your initial monthly payment figure due to information available after the closing of your loan.

Engages the services of   as its servicer. You will be receiving a billing notice from   within two weeks of your loan funding.   has the right to collect your payments and this in no way affects the terms and conditions of the mortgage instruments, other than the terms directly related to the servicing of your loan. If you do not receive a payment booklet or have other questions about the servicing of your loan, please call:

Please send your payments to:

Any correspondence, or calls, in reference to your loan, please refer to the above loan number. However, your loan number will be changed for servicing purposes.

Copy received and acknowledged.

Figure 10:10 Sample Mailing Address Confirmation

The buyer will often be asked to sign a statement confirming their mailing address and understanding of the monthly payment dictated through the mortgage and note documents. This statement will

- Detail the correspondence information of the borrower

- State the monthly payment breakdown specifics including breakdown information for PMI, school and county taxes, insurance premiums and any reserves required under the mortgage agreement

- Define any mortgage servicing information known to the mortgage lender at the time of closing

- Detail the mailing address and other contact information of the mortgage lender

The borrower will be asked to review all of the entries on this document and confirm a receipt of a copy of the statement. The mailing address and payment confirmation is a snapshot of all of the data pertaining to the loan that was included on the previous pages and it is critical that you ensure the borrower receives a copy of this statement in their closing package.

A sample HUD 1 Settlement Statement is included in a later chapter for your review. The entries on the HUD 1 will come from a variety of sources including

- Sales Agreement and Addendums

- Payoff Statements

- Earnest Money Deposit Funds

- Lenders Instructions

- Service Billings

- Pro-rata Calculations

- and any other financial document applicable to the transaction.

You should review the lender inclusions to determine if there are any additional or incorrectly applied items. The lender may also detail items that they require to have added or modified on the HUD 1. Any changes or variations discovered should be confirmed with the applicable parties prior to the generation of the final document for signing at the closing.

> Example: A common alteration to the HUD 1 Settlement Statement that might occur due to lender instructions is the requirement that the buyer pay off specific debt in order to gain final approval for the new home mortgage.
>
> If the closing agent did not calculate this debt as part of the funds required of the buyer at closing, the HUD 1 would be incorrect.
>
> It is important to verify every figure entered on the HUD 1 against the applicable billings, instructions and negotiated documents before the closing begins. This assists you in isolating any issues before the signing and aids in smoothing the closing process for all parties.

The closing instructions received from the lender will typically provide more transaction details than any other document you receive except the Real Estate Sales Agreement. It is important that you understand the entries on the Lenders Closing Instructions. The following pages will provide you with an example of an actual series of instructions received from a lender for the closing of a mortgage loan. You should familiarize yourself with the entries detailed as well as the blank entries on each form. Any item incorporated into the lender's closing instructions will affect the closing. A large portion of your settlement duties will be to meet the requirements of the lender.

MORTGAGE DOCUMENTS

Financing transactions that contain real estate are typically secured using a mortgage.

- A mortgage causes the note to be secured against real property rather than other property or as an unsecured personal loan.

Typically, a seller or lender will utilize both a note and a mortgage in these types of financing situations.

- The note is the promise to repay the funds detailed in the manner detailed.

- A mortgage is a separate agreement from the note and provides the security or collateral of the real property involved in the transaction in the event of non-payment on the part of the buyer.

In addition to the legal form of a mortgage, two key components will often be incorporated into the document.

- the act of putting the property as collateral in return for the funds being provided will be detailed

- the conditions under which the buyer will maintain the collateral to protect the interest of the lender until the terms of the note are satisfied and all funds are paid will be outlined

Mortgage Key

A legal mortgage document may vary in appearance from the sample included for your review. As with all closing documents, the inclusions of the mortgage agreement will vary depending on the specific negotiations between the parties. In general, you can expect to find the following specific items in a mortgage.

- The date of the making or signing of the mortgage agreement

- The names of the parties involved in the mortgage including both the borrower and the lender

  Mortgagor is the person who owes the mortgage or borrower

  Mortgagee is the person who is receiving the payments or the lender

- The debt for which the mortgage is being held as collateral is named.

- The borrower of the funds conveys the property being held as collateral to the lender.

- The mortgaged property is then described.

- The borrower states that the property being provided as collateral legally belongs to them and that the borrower will be responsible for defending ownership against all other claims of interest by other properties.

  The seller or lender will want to verify this claim by the buyer through a title search and, at times, require the buyer to carry title insurance as a combat against any future claims to the title by other parties.

- A defeasance clause will be incorporated.

  This clause outlines the provisions to nullify and make void the mortgage when the note has been paid in full.

- The borrower makes certain promises to the lender, which protect the collateral or property, which acts as security for the loan.

Covenant to Pay Taxes	The borrower agrees to pay the property taxes on the mortgaged property.
	This is an important factor for the lender because if the taxes are not paid they may create a lien on the property, which is superior to the lien held by the lender.
Covenant Against Removal	The borrower is prohibited from removing or demolishing any building or improvement on the property.
	Demolishing or removing improvements may reduce the value of the collateral offered to the lender against the note.
Covenant of Insurance	The borrower is required to carry adequate homeowners insurance to protect the lender interest in the collateral in the event of the damage or destruction of a part of the property.
Covenant of Good Repair	The borrower must keep the collateral in good condition.
	This is also sometimes referred to as the covenant of preservation and maintenance.
	A clause providing the lender with the right to inspect the property to ensure it is being maintained in a manner, which protects the value

of the collateral given to the lender, is often incorporated into the mortgage.

Acceleration clause   The acceleration clause permits the lender to demand all monies owed as payable immediately.

If the borrower cannot pay the money owed in full a foreclosure proceeding, is implemented and the property is sold with the lender receiving monies from the sale to pay the funds owed.

This clause is used if the borrower breaks any clause included in the agreement.

Alienation clause or
due-on-sale clause   This clause allows the lender to call the entire loan   balance as due if the property is sold or conveyed by the borrower to another individual.

If any part of all of the property is taken by the act of eminent domain this clause provides the lender with the right to receive any money paid as part of the action to offset the balance of the loan owed.

- A section will be incorporated that states the borrower has created this mortgage. The signature of the borrower fulfills the same requirement.

- The borrower will acknowledge the mortgage by the signing of the document.

   As the settlement agent, you must witness this signature, confirm the identity of the signor and confirm that the signature matches the printed name exactly as it appears within the document.

When a note or loan is paid in full, the lender will typically return the promissory note to the borrower. The lender will also provide the borrower with a satisfaction of mortgage document that states the promissory note has been paid in full. This allows the mortgage to be discharged from the public records. It is important that this document be recorded by the public recorder in the same county in which the original mortgage document was recorded.

ASSUMPTION

At times, the seller may have secured a mortgage on a property that allows for the assumption of the mortgage by another party.

- This means the buyer will sign documents with the mortgage holder to take over the position of the seller in the mortgage transaction.

In this scenario, the mortgage holder made a mortgage loan to the seller during a previous transaction. By signing assumptions documents presented by the lender, the buyer effectively takes the seller's place in the mortgage and note agreements and removes the seller's obligations to pay the mortgage holder.

- The terms of the mortgage that the buyer is assuming will remain the same.

This assumption is sometimes attractive to a buyer, especially when the mortgage that the seller is holding carries better interest rates and terms than the current market could offer the buyer if a new mortgage loan was secured. Not all mortgages are assumable. The ability to perform this type of transfer depends on the terms the original lender set.

The seller should read their mortgage documents carefully to determine if this is a potential option. In the event the mortgage may be assumed by a new buyer, the lender or mortgage holder will usually require the buyer to meet certain eligibility criteria.

Even when the existing mortgage is assumed, the seller may require additional funds from the buyer towards the purchase of the property. These additional funds are typically equal to the amount of equity (value – mortgage = equity) the seller holds in the property.

Because a conventional lender is involved, there may be certain minimum requirements set forth concerning the amount of cash a new borrower must invest up front or the maximum amount of a second mortgage the seller may hold against the property. These issues should be discussed with a loan officer from the original lending institution and then negotiated, according to the original lender restrictions, between the buyer and the seller.

An example of a simplified clause negotiating the assumption plus a cash balance owed in one lump sum is detailed on the following page. A variation of this clause may be created if the buyer and seller agree that the seller will receive their cash portion of the sales price in monthly payments or another negotiated term and held by a 2nd mortgage and note. This example form is a broad form and as always, the services of a real estate attorney or other competent professional should be retained when creating any contract. As the settlement agent, you will witness the acknowledgements of this document but should refer any questions pertaining to the inclusions to the individual or company that generated the document.

LOAN ASSUMPTION ADDENDUM

TO CONTRACT CONCERNING THE PROPERTY AT: (Address of Property)

_____

A.   CREDIT DOCUMENTATION: Within _____ days after the effective date of this contract,

Purchaser shall deliver to Seller the following: (check all applicable items

_____ Credit report

_____ Verification of employment, including salary

_____ Verification of funds on deposit in financial institutions

_____ Current financial statement to establish Purchaser's creditworthiness

_____ Other: _____

Purchaser hereby authorizes any credit-reporting agency to furnish to Seller at Purchaser's sole   expense copies of Purchaser's credit reports. _____ Signature

B.   CREDIT APPROVAL: If Purchaser's documentation is not delivered within the specified time, Seller may terminate this contract by notice to Purchaser within 7 days after expiration of the time for delivery, and the earnest money will be paid to Seller.

If the documentation is timely delivered, and Seller determines in Seller's sole discretion that Purchaser's credit is unacceptable, Seller may terminate this contract by notice to Purchaser within 7 days after expiration of the time for delivery and the earnest money will be refunded to Purchaser.

If Seller does not terminate this contract, Seller will be deemed to have accepted Purchaser's   credit.

C.   ASSUMPTION:

_____ (1)   The unpaid principal balance of a first lien promissory note payable to which unpaid balance at closing will be $_____. The total current monthly payment including principal, interest and any reserve deposits is $_____. Purchaser's initial payment will be the first payment due after closing.

_____ (2)   The unpaid principal balance of a second lien promissory note payable to which unpaid balance at closing will be $_____. The total current monthly payment including principal, interest and any reserve deposits is $_____. Purchaser's initial payment will be the first payment due after closing.

Purchaser's assumption of an existing note includes all obligations imposed by the deed of trust securing the note. If the unpaid principal balance(s) of any assumed loan(s) as of the Closing Date varies from the loan balance(s) stated above, the (check only one)

Figure 10:26 Sample Assumption Addendum – Page 1

D.   Cash payable at closing

Sales Price will be adjusted by the amount of any variance; provided, if the total principal balance of all assumed loans varies in an amount greater than $350.00 at closing, either party may terminate this contract and the earnest money will be refunded to Purchaser unless the other party elects to eliminate the excess in the variance by an appropriate adjustment at closing.   Purchaser may terminate this contract and the earnest money will be refunded to Purchaser if the note holder requires

1.   payment of an assumption fee in excess of $_____ in (A) above or $_____ in (2) above and Seller declines to pay such excess, an increase in the interest rate to more than _____% in (1) above, or _____% in (B) above, any other modification of the loan documents, or consent to the assumption of the loan and fails to consent.

2.   An appropriate instrument authorized within the state, typically either

(A) a mortgage or

(B) Vendor's and deed of trust liens,

To secure the assumption will be required, and it will automatically be released on execution and delivery of a release by note holder. If Seller is released from liability on any assumed note, the instrument securing the assumption will not be required. If note holder maintains an escrow account, the escrow account must be transferred to Purchaser without any deficiency. Purchaser shall reimburse Seller for the amount in the transferred accounts.

E.   NOTICE TO PURCHASER: The monthly payments, interest rates or other terms of some loans may be adjusted by the note holder at or after closing. If you are concerned about the possibility of future adjustments, do not sign the contract without examining the notes and   the instrument securing the note.

F.   NOTICE TO SELLER: Your liability to pay the note assumed by Purchaser will continue unless you obtain a release of liability from the note holder. If you are concerned about future liability, you should use a Release of Liability Addendum.

PURCHASER:

_____
Date

_____
Purchaser Signature

_____
Printed Name

SELLER:

_____
Date

_____
Seller Signature

_____
Printed Name

Figure 10:27 Sample Assumption Addendum – Page 2

MORTGAGE ASSUMPTION AGREEMENT

THIS MORTGAGE ASSUMPTION AGREEMENT (hereinafter referred to as the "Agreement") made and entered into as of this __ day of _____, 20__, by and between _____, of _____, (hereinafter referred to as the "Lender") and _____, of _____ (hereinafter referred to as "Borrower").

W I T N E S S E T H:

WHEREAS, Lender is the holder and owner of the following documents (hereinafter sometimes collectively referred to as the "Loan Documents"):

1. Mortgage Note dated _____, in the original principal face amount of _____ DOLLARS ($_____) executed and delivered by _____ (hereinafter referred to as the "Original Borrower") in favor of Lender   (hereinafter referred to as the "Note"); and,

2. Mortgage given by Original Borrower as "Mortgagor" to Lender as "Mortgagee" dated _____, which Mortgage is recorded on the Public Records of _____ County, _____ at O.R. Book __, Page __ (hereinafter referred to as the "Mortgage"), and which Mortgage encumbers the real property as described therein; and,

WHEREAS, the Original Borrower is desirous of conveying the property encumbered by the Mortgage, (hereinafter referred to as the "Property") to Borrower; and,

WHEREAS, the Borrower desires to receive said Property and formally assume the Mortgage and perform all of the covenants and conditions contained in the Mortgage Note, the Mortgage and all other Loan Documents as partial consideration for its purchase of the Property and as consideration for the Lender's willingness to consent to the sale of the Property which is encumbered by the Loan Documents; and,

WHEREAS, the Mortgage expressly prohibits the conveyance of the Property without the express written consent of the Lender; and,

WHEREAS, the Lender is unwilling to give its consent to the transfer of the Property to the Borrower unless the Borrower shall assume all of the obligations heretofore imposed by the Loan Documents upon the Original Borrower;

NOW, THEREFORE, for and in consideration of the sum of _____DOLLARS ($_____) and in consideration of the Premises and of the mutual covenants contained herein, and for other good and valuable considerations, the receipt and sufficiency of which are hereby acknowledged by the parties, the parties hereto agree as follows:

1. Assumption. Borrower expressly assumes the Loan Documents, agrees to perform all covenants, conditions, duties and obligations contained therein, and agrees to pay the Note and the obligations evidenced thereby in a prompt and timely manner in accordance with the terms thereof.

2. Consent to Conveyance. Lender hereby consents to the transfer of the Property to the Borrower, but the Lender expressly reserves the right to withhold its consent to any future sale or transfer of the Property, as provided for in the Mortgage.

Figure 10:28 Sample Assumption Agreement – Page 1

3.   Warranties and Representations. Borrower affirms warrants, represents and covenants that Borrower has neither defenses nor rights of set-off against Lender or against the payment, collection or enforcement of the indebtedness evidenced by the Note and secured by the Mortgage and owed to Lender. Borrower further warrants and represents as follows:

a. Borrower has done no acts nor omitted to do any act which might prevent Lender from, or limit Lender in, acting upon or under any of the provisions herein, in the Mortgage, in the Note or any other Loan Documents

b. Borrower is not prohibited under any other agreement with any other person or any judgment or decree, from the execution and delivery of this Agreement, the performance of each and every covenant hereunder or under the Mortgage, Note or any other Loan Documents

c. No action has been brought or threatened which would in any way interfere with the right of Borrower to execute this Agreement and perform all of Borrower's obligations contained herein, in the Note, in the Mortgage, or in any other Loan Document

d. All financial statements of Borrower and Guarantors, if any, are true and correct in all respects, fairly present the respective financial conditions of the subjects thereof, as of the respective dates thereof and no material adverse change has occurred that would affect Borrower's or Guarantors', if any, ability to repay the indebtedness evidenced by the Note and   secured by the Mortgage

e. Borrower is duly formed, validly existing and in good standing under the laws of the State of _____ and has full power and authority to consummate the transactions contemplated under this Agreement.

4.   Acknowledgements. Borrower acknowledges that:

a. The Loan Documents are in full force and effect; and,

b. The principal balance of the loan as represented by the aforesaid Note as of the date of this Agreement is _____ DOLLARS ($_____) and principal and interest are   unconditionally due and owing to the Lender as provided in the Note.

5.   Costs. Borrower shall pay all costs of the assumption made hereby, to include without limitation, attorneys' fees and recording costs, as well as the cost of an endorsement to Lender's title insurance policy insuring the lien of the Mortgage after the recording of this Agreement. Such costs shall be due at closing hereunder and the payment thereof shall be a condition precedent to Lender's consent to the transfer of the Property to Borrower. In the event that it is determined that additional costs relating to this transaction are due, Borrower agrees to pay such costs immediately upon demand.

6.   Assumption Fee. In consideration of Lender's consenting to the conveyance of the Property to the Borrower, Lender is entitled to, and has earned, an assumption fee in the amount of __ percent (___%) of the original principal face amount of the indebtedness evidenced by the Note. Said fee shall be due and payable upon the execution and delivery of this Agreement. Borrower hereby agrees and acknowledges that said fee is being charged solely for costs relating to the assumption of the Mortgage and not as interest for the forbearance or use of money.

7.   Recordation. The recording of this Agreement on the Public Records shall evidence the closing of the transaction described herein.

Figure 10:29 Sample Assumption Agreement – Page 2

8.   Paragraph Headings. The paragraph headings used herein are for convenience of reference only and shall not be used in the interpretation or construction hereof.

9.   Governing Law. This Agreement shall be governed, interpreted and construed by, through and under the laws of the State of _____.

10.   Time of the Essence. Time is of the essence of this Agreement.

11.   Attorneys' Fees. All costs incurred by Lender in enforcing this Agreement and in collection of sums due Lender from Borrower, to include, without limitation, reasonable attorneys' fees through all trials, appeals, and proceedings, to include, without limitation, any proceedings pursuant to the bankruptcy laws of the United States and any arbitration proceedings, shall be paid by Borrower.

12.   Binding Effect. This Agreement shall inure to the benefit of and be binding upon the parties   hereto as well as their successors and assigns, heirs and personal representatives.

IN WITNESS WHEREOF, the parties hereto have duly executed this Agreement as follows:

As to Lender this ____ day of _____, 20_____.

"LENDER"   WITNESSES:

_____   _____

As to Borrower this day of _____, 20_____.

"BORROWER"   WITNESSES:

_____   _____

Figure 10:30 Sample Assumption Agreement – Page 3

CHAPTER
11

VERIFICATIONS AND CERTIFICATIONS

Many closings will require the confirmation of other documents beyond what has been detailed in the previous chapters. The most common documents that you will encounter are detailed on the following pages. You should familiarize yourself with the appearance, inclusions and form of each of these documents.

Remember that the inclusions are the most common appearances you will encounter but that each form may be customized by the individual or company preparing the documents and so the actual format at your closing may vary from the examples.

Each section is described and you should understand the reason for inclusion in a closing package and the applicable actions you must take to obtain correct acknowledgement for each document. Remember you are acting as a witness to the transaction rather than a legal advisor.

If any questions pertaining to any document should arise during the settlement meeting, you should direct the question to the company or individual who created the applicable signature requirement. If there is no company or individual available to answer any questions that arise, the services of a competent attorney should be obtained to gain the needed clarification.

REAL ESTATE CLOSING - SETTLEMENT AGENT

ITEMIZATION OF AMOUNT FINANCED

Borrower   Creditor:

Loan Number: Date:

Property Address: Term:
                                            Rate:
                                            LTV:

Listed below is the ITEMIZATION OF AMOUNT FINANCED.

Existing Lien: $
Loan Amount $

ITEMIZATION OF PRPAID FINANCE CHARGES:

    -- Origination Points   to LENDER
    -- Lender Discount Points   to LENDER
    -- Administration Fee to LENDER
    -- Prepaid Interest for
    -- Settlement or Closing Fee to

        TOTAL PREPAID FINANCE CHARGE: $_____
        AMOUNT FINANCED: $

OTHER SETTLEMENT CHARGES:
    AMOUNTS PAID TO OTHERS ON YOUR
    BEHALF BY CREDITOR

    -- Lender Appraisal Fee to
    -- Abstract or Title Search to
    -- Notary Fee to
    -- Title Insurance to
    -- Recording Fee (Deed: $)

        TOTAL OTHER SETTLEMENT CHARGE: $_____

        LOAN PROCEEDS: $_____

FEES PAID BY LENDER

        TOTAL FEES PAID BY LENDER: $_____

I (We) hereby acknowledge that I (we) have received and read a completed copy of the HUD Special Information Booklet "Settlement Cost", unless the loan being applied is for refinancing the property.

If for any reason the loan I (we) have applied for does not close, and if permitted by applicable law, I (we) agree to reimburse the lender for any and all costs incurred to process my (our) application including, but not limited to: appraisal, survey, and title insurance.

Figure 11:1 Sample Itemization of Amount Financed

While some of the inclusions contained in the itemization of the amount financed may be the same as those appearing on the HUD 1 Settlement Statement or the instructions of costs from the lender, others will not be included on these documents.

The Itemization of Amount Financed is a different document and should not be used in the creation of or incorporated into the Settlement Statement. This document is intended as a legal disclosure document from the lender to the borrower of funds. This disclosure will include items paid by the lender on the borrower's behalf and then financed as a part of the transaction.

CORRECTION AGREEMENT
LIMITED POWER OF ATTORNEY

On   , the undersigned Borrower(s), for and in consideration of the approval, closing and funding of their mortgage loan (No.   ) hereby grant
as settlement agent and/or   as Lender limited power of attorney to correct and/or execute or initial all typographical or clerical errors discovered in any or all of the closing documentation required to be executed by the undersigned at settlement. In the even this limited power of attorney is exercised, the undersigned will be notified and receive a copy of the document executed or initialed on their behalf.

THIS LIMITED POWER OF ATTORNEY MAY NOT BE USED TO INCREASE THE INTERST RATE (NOR THE MARGIN OR INDEX FOR VARIABLE RATE LOANS) THE UNDERSIGNED IS PAYING, INCREASE THE TERM OF THE UDNERSIGNED'S LOAN, INCREASE THE UDNERSIGNED'S OUTSTANDING PRINCIPAL BALANCE OR INCREASE THE UNDERSIGNED'S MONTHLY PRINCIPAL AND INTEREST PAYMENTS. Any of these specified changes must be executed directly by the undersigned.

This Limited Power of Attorney shall automatically terminate 180 days from the closing date of the undersigned's mortgage loan.

Figure 11:2 Sample Correction Agreement

At times, after the closing is complete, a typographical or specific clerical error may be discovered in the fully executed documents. Rather than return to the signor and request a new signature, a limited power of attorney is often executed at the closing. This limited power of attorney provides for specific individuals to correct the typographical or clerical errors on behalf of the signor.

This authorization expressly states that the signor will receive a copy of all altered documentation.

The authorization also specifically excludes alterations to the index or margin of an adjustable rate loan, interest rate, term, principal balance, or principal and interest payment.

The limited power of attorney will also contain a specific end date for the authorizations granted.

Date:

Lender:

Borrower(s):

Loan Number:

Property Address:

WARRANTY AND COMPLIANCE AGREEMENT

In order to induce the lender to make the above loan and in consideration thereof, the undersigned borrower(s):

1.   Warrants and represents to the lender that all information it or its agents have provided to the lender, including without limitation all information contained in the loan application and all documents associated therewith, is true and accurate in all respects as of the date below. In making this statement, the borrower understands that (a) the lender has relied on the accuracy of such information in its decision to make the loan, and (b) if any such information is inaccurate, the lender or its assignee may foreclose or cancel the loan and pursue other legal remedies, including damages for fraud UNDER THE PROVISIONS OF THE DEED OF TRUST, ITEM 6.

2.   Agrees that if any document evidencing the loan does not correctly or accurately reflect the terms of loans offered by lender in the program under which the undersigned applied, including, but not lmited to, maturity date, interest rate, refinance options, etc., or is not on a form approved for such program as a result of a mistake or clerical error by lender, whether such mistake or error is mutual or unknown to the undersigned, the undersigned will:

(a)   execute and/or initial modifications, amendments, or replacement documents as necessary to accurately and correctly reflect the terms of the loan or to ensure the loan is evidenced by the proper documentation; and

(b)   take such other actions as the lender may reasonably request under the circumstances to   correct such mistake or clerical error.

In this connection, the undersigned acknowledges that the lender is a mortgage banker which only makes loans that meet criteria established and/or approved by secondary market investors to whom many of the loans it makes are ultimately sold. The undersigned further understands that the lender only offers loan programs which are approved by such investors or meet their established criteria, that any failure to perform the covenants and promises set forth in this agreement may render a loan unmarketable and thereby result in loss or damage to the lender, and that the undersigned's execution of this agreement and willingness to perform obligations assumed herein are material to the lender's decision to make the loan.

Figure 11:3 Sample Warranty and Compliance Notice

The borrower will be asked to confirm or warranty that all of the information provided to the mortgage lender during the loan application is correct. This document will specify that the borrower is guaranteeing that they have provided only accurate statements in association with the loan application and will state that the borrower agrees that penalties may be invoked if any information provided is found to be untrue.

The document will also detail for the borrower the steps that they must take if they find an error or discrepancy in the mortgage documents.

You will be asked to notarize the signatures on this document. It is very important that you confirm that all of the signatures affixed to the document match the loan paperwork exactly as it appears. This document is critical to the mortgage lenders position and an incomplete or inaccurate signature could become an issue if an error in the paperwork of the loan becomes apparent at some point in the future.

TAX CERTIFICATE

Loan / Contract #
Loan Name:
Loan State
Division:
Address:
Jurisdiction:
Date Added: Date Completed
Refresh Requested: Refresh Completed:
$ Tax Jurisdictions: # Real Parcels:

                        Parcel #   Control $
YES Delinquent Taxes.
No Exemptions:
Delinquent Amount:

SUMMARY

Jurisdiction	Parcel #	Tax Year	Tax Amount	Due Date*	Paid

* The Due Date listed is the last day to make payment before there are additional penalties and/or interest added to the amount to be paid. In the case of a Discount Due Date, the date is the last day to make payment before the amount to be paid is the next discount amount listed or gross tax listed to be paid.

Figure 11:4 Sample Tax Certificate

A tax certificate will be obtained on all closings. The lender will often require a copy of the tax certificate as part of the closing instructions that must be carried out in order to obtain the final funding of a mortgage loan.

A tax certificate searches the applicable tax records for the subject property being closed to determine the current payment status.

If taxes are paid in full, the tax certificate will indicate said payment status.

If there are taxes that are in a delinquency status, the tax certificate will detail

- the exact payment amount

- the date that the tax billing became delinquent

- the taxing authority to which the applicable taxes are owed

Unless an agreement between the parties exists which dictates that these taxes may remain unpaid, all tax billings must be paid current at the time of the closing. A mortgage lender will typically require full payment regardless of any other agreements.

BORROWER(S):

PROPERTY ADDRES:

NON IMPOUND NOTICE

I DO UNDERSTAND THAT THE LENDER FOR THIS MORTGAGE WILL NOT IMPOUND FOR REAL ESTATE TAXES AND HOMEOWNERS INSURANCE COVERAGE ON THE ABOVE REFERENCED ACCOUNT.

THE MONTHLY PAYMENT I WILL BE MAKING ONLY COVERS PRINCIPAL AND INTEREST ON THE LOAN.

I AM FULLY RESPONSIBLE TO PAY FOR REAL ESTATE TAXES AND HOMEOWNERS INSURACE POLICY PREMIUMS WHEN THEY BECOME PAYABLE.

Figure 11:5 Sample Non Impound Notice

The buyer and lender will negotiate the manner in which taxes, insurance and other recurring outside billings will be handled.

- At times, the buyer will pay a portion of these bills to the lender with each monthly payment.

  The lender will then hold the portional payments in an escrow account until the billings become due.

The lender then makes payment for these billings.

- At other times, the buyer may agree to pay the billings as they become due.

This is known as impounding, not impounding, escrowing, or not escrowing payments.

Whichever method is chosen, a document will often be presented at closing that details the choices, handling and confirms the actions required of each party. You must obtain the proper signature on these documents, as the payment of such billings can be critical to maintaining the rights of the parties in the transaction.

The Federal Truth in Lending disclosure or TIL is another document that contains financial figures with which you should be familiar but will not be incorporated into the Settlement Statement. The purpose of the TIL is to disclose to the borrower the true cost of the credit that they are obtaining. The TIL will incorporate any costs that are not readily apparent in the buyer's interest rate or settlement statement. While you should become familiar with the format and inclusions of the TIL, you should direct any questions that a buyer might have pertaining to the document to the Mortgage Lender, Loan Processor or Closing Team that generated the document.

The lender may be subject to random file reviews or may have need to confirm the information contained within the buyer's application, loan package and tax documents at some time in the future. This could occur for a variety of reasons such as the packaging of loans to sell on the secondary mortgage market, standard lender reviews or servicing transfers. Regardless of the reason, many Mortgage Lenders require documents in the file that allow them to access and verify certain borrower records. The closing agent will be responsible for providing these documents to the buyer for review and signature. It is important that you confirm that all forms required on the lender closing instructions are included in the loan package prior to beginning the settlement meeting. You should also verify that all required documents are completed prior to concluding the meeting.

REAL ESTATE CLOSING - SETTLEMENT AGENT

FEDERAL TRUTH-IN-LENDING DISCLOSURE STATEMENT

Borrower   Creditor

Loan Number   Date

ANNUAL PERCENTAGE RATE The cost of your credit as a yearly rate.	FINANCE CHARGE The dollar amount the credit will cost you.	Amount Financed The amount of credit provided to you or on you behalf	Total of Payments The amount you will have paid after you have made all payments as scheduled

Your payment schedule will be:

No. of Pmts.	Amount of Pmts.	Monthly Pmts. Begin	No. of Pmts	Amount of Pmts.	Monthly Pmts Begin	No. of Pmts.	Amount of Pmts.	Monthly Pmts. Begin

THIS IS AN INTEREST ONLY LOAN, THE FIRST 120 PAYMENTS ARE INTEREST ONLY. THIS LOAN
WILL CONTAIN A PREPAYMENT PENALTY FOR 36 MONTHS

11:9 Example Federal TIL Statement – HUD Release

USE OF YOUR TELEPHONE,
FACSIMILE AND CELLULAR TELEPHONE NUMBERS

Date:

Borrower(s):   Lender:

Property Address:

Please provide the following information:

Home Telephone Number   (_____) _____   (_____) _____

Work Telephone Number   (_____) _____   (_____) _____

Cellular Telephone Number (_____) _____   (_____) _____

Facsimile Number   (_____) _____   (_____) _____

Email Address   _____   _____

Name of closest relative _____   _____

Relative's Telephone   (_____) _____   (_____) _____

By signing below, Borrower agrees that the lender, lender's affiliates, the loan servicer and their respective successors and assigns (collectively "we" may contact you at the telephone numbers and email addresses listed above for any purpose related to the servicing and collection of any loan(s) or line of credit we have made to you. You agree that we may use automated dialing and announcing devices to make such calls and that we may contact you at any telephone, facsimile, cellular telephone number, or email address that we may subsequently obtain.

Figure 11:9 Sample Contact Information Request

When credit is provided, it is becoming a common practice for a lender to obtain all possible contact information for the borrower. They may also request the contact information of individuals who might assist in locating the borrower in the event an issue arises with the repayment of the borrower funds. Many individuals have multiple means of contact and all of them will be requested.

If the borrower's contact information is requested during the closing, specific authorizations as to how the lender may use that contact information will often be incorporated into the request. If such a document is provided for completion at a closing you are officiating, you should present it to the applicable signor for completion. All fields should be completed by the signor. You are to act only as a witness to the completion.

CREDIT BUREAU NOTICE TO THE HOME APPLICANT

Empirica

_____
current score   date of score

Key Factors:

Equifax

_____
current score   date of score

Key Factors

Experian

_____
current score   date of score

Key Factors

In connection with your application for a home loan, we must disclose to you the score that a credit bureau distributed to users and in connection with your home loan and the key factors affecting your credit score.

The credit score is a computer generate summary calculated at the time of the request and based on information a credit bureau or lender has on file. The scores are based on data about your credit history and payment patterns. Credit scores are important because they are used to assist the lender in determining whether you will obtain a loan. They may also be used to determine what interest rate may be offered on the mortgage. Credit scores can change over time depending on your conduct, how your credit history and payment patterns change, and how credit-scoring technologies change.

Because the score is based on information in your credit history, it is very important that you review the credit-related information that is being furnished to make sure it is accurate. Credit records may vary from one company to another.

If you have questions about your score or the credit information that is furnished to you, contact the credit bureau at the address and telephone number provided in this notice. The credit bureau generated this score. The credit bureau plays no part in the decision to take action on the loan application and is unable to provide you with specific reasons for the decision on the loan application..

Figure 11:10 Sample Credit Bureau Notice

When funds are lent as part of a transaction, the basis for the lending parameters is often the credit report. When the credit report plays a role in the funds obtained, a disclosure will be provided explaining

- the scores received from the bureaus

- the factors contributing to the scores

- the fact that the bureaus do not make a credit determination but rather report the inclusions of the credit profile

KENNEY

Contact information and directions to inquire into the credit profile will often be incorporated into the disclosure.

Lender/Creditor: Loan No.:

GENERAL AUTHORIZATION AND BORROWER'S CERTIFICATION

CERTIFICATION

The Undersigned certify the following:

1. I/We have applied for a mortgage loan from Lender. In applying for the loan, I/we completed a loan application containing various information on the purpose of the loan, the amount and source of the down payment, employment and income information, and assets and liabilities. I/We certify that all of the information is true and complete. I/We made no misrepresentations in the loan application or other documents, nor did I/we omit any pertinent information.

2. I/We understand and agree that in the event the loan is processed under a reduced documentation program, Lender reserves the right to change the mortgage loan review process to a full documentation program. This may include verifying the information provided on the application with the employer and/or financial institution.

3. I/We fully understand that it is a Federal crime punishable by fine, or imprisonment, or both to knowingly make any false statements when applying for this mortgage, as applicable under the provisions of Title 18, United States Code, Section 1014.

AUTHORIZATION TO RELEASE INFORMATION

1. I/We have applied for a mortgage loan from Lender. As part of the application process, Lender may verify information contained in my/our loan application and in other documents required in connection with the loan, either before the loan is closed or as part of its quality control program.

2. I/We authorize you to provide to Lender, and to any investor to whom Lender may sell my mortgage, any and all information and documentation that they request. Such information includes but is not limited to, employment history and income; bank, money market, and similar account balances; credit history; and copies of income tax returns.

3. Lender or any investor that purchases the mortgage may address this authorization to any party named in the loan application.

4. A copy of this authorization may be accepted as the original.

5. Your prompt reply to Lender or the investor that purchased the mortgage is appreciated.

Figure 11:11 Sample General Authorization

Whenever information is gathered including credit reports, employment history, financial institution data and tax return information a release for such information gathering must be completed by the subject of the search. During the transaction, a potential lender will obtain such release signatures but will often require that another release be signed at the closing table. You should have the borrower in question complete the form and sign all documents. Your job in this instance is only to present said forms for completion.

Additional verifications must be completed pertaining to the identity of the individuals singing at the closing.

If a mortgage loan is to be a part of the closing, these validations of identity will often be required as part of the closing instructions.

If no mortgage loan is included in the transaction, you will still be required to verify the identity of each party so that you can confirm, if necessary, that all documents are legally binding on the parties to the transaction through the signature.

To verify the identity of each party, you will need to obtain valid photo identification from each signor. You may also be required to have applicable parties to the transaction complete signature affidavit documents and other items. Some examples of the forms that may be required are included on the following pages for review. Again, you should familiarize yourself with the applicable document but refer any questions pertaining to the need for or inclusions within each document to the applicable service provider.

You, as the settlement agent will complete a form that confirms that you have reviewed the applicable identity documents and verified that the individual signing are who they claim.

ACKNOWLEDGEMENT

STATE OF   _____

COUNTY OF   _____

On _____ before me, _____, PERSONALLY APPEARED
     (DATE)   NAME, TITLE OFFIER E.G. NOTARY PUBLIC

_____

_____
NAME(S) OF SIGNERS

_____ Personally known to me –or- _____ proved to me on the basis of satisfactory evidence to be the person(s) whose name(s) is/are subscribed to the within instrument and acknowledged to me that he/she/ they executed the same in his/her/their authorized capacity(ies), and that by his/her/their signature(s) on the instrument the person(s), or the entity upon behalf of which the person(s) acted, executed the instrument.

WITNESS my hand and official seal,

_____

SIGNATURE OF NOTARY

MY COMMISSION EXPIRES ON:

Description of Attached Document:

Title to Type of Document: _____

Document Date: _____   Number of Pages: _____

Signors Other Than Named Above: _____

Figure 11:13 Sample Acknowledgement

IDENTIFICATION VALIDATION ACKNOWLEDGEMENT
(This document should be used by the Closing Agent)
(Required when no photo copy of I.D. is available)

Borrower Name(s):

Loan Number:

In accordance with the USA Patriot Act, the following documentation was reviewed to verify the identity of the customer:

___ State issued Driver's License

B1#_____   Exp Date: _____

B2#_____   Exp Date: _____

B3#_____   Exp Date: _____

B4#_____   Exp Date: _____

__   Passport

B1#_____   B2#_____

B3#_____   B4#_____

__   Other (Please describe)

_____

_____

B1#_____   B2#_____

B3#_____   B4#_____

By signing below, the closing agent acknowledges that they have reviewed the above documentation and have verified the identification of the borrowers listed above.

Figure 11:14 Sample Identity Verification

IMPORTANT INFORMATION ABOUT
PROCEDURES FOR YOUR NEW LOAN REQUEST

To help the government fight the funding of terrorism and money laundering activities, Federal law requires all financial institutions to obtain, verify, and record information that identifies each person who opens an account.

What this means for you: When you open an account, we will ask for your name, address, date of birth, business documents, and other information that will allow us to identify you. We may also ask to see your driver's license or other identifying documents.

Figure 11:15 Sample Terrorism Notice

SIGNATURE AFFADAVIT AND AKA STATEMENT

I certify that this is my true and correct signature:

_____   _____
Borrower   Sample Signature

AKA STATEMENT

I further certify that I am also known as:

_____   _____
Name Variation (Print)   Sample Signature (Variation)

_____   _____
Name Variation (Print)   Sample Signature (Variation)

_____   _____
Name Variation (Print)   Sample Signature (Variation)

Figure 11:16 Sample Signature Affidavit

The signature affidavit will be a sampling of possible signatures of the buyer. This document is often requested when names other than the one under which the loan is being granted appear on the credit report. Examples of when a signature affidavit would be important include:

- A married woman who previously obtained credit under her maiden name would be asked to sign the form using the maiden name as well as the married name.

- An individual whose credit report shows credit was obtained using a nickname or shortened name for example Samuel could have obtained credit as Sam so both name variations would be included in the signature section.

- An individual may have obtained some credit using their middle initial while other credit entries could have been obtained without the middle initial included. A signature with and without the middle initial would be requested.

- A typographical or clerical error might have been entered when a credit entry was made. This typographical error would appear on the credit report so the signor would be asked to provide a signature using the incorrect entry name.

- Any other matter that shows on the credit report indicating that a name variation exists would be cause for an entry on the signature affidavit form.

CLOSING VALIDATION

Please acknowledge receipt of all enclosures and your complete understanding of our instructions and conditions by signing and returning the instructions.

Closing Agent Acknowledgement: _____ Date: _____

_____   _____

_____   _____

_____   _____

Please forward final Title Policy and Recorded Deed of Trust to:

Figure 11:17 Sample Closing Validation

Upon completion of all tasks set forth on the lender instruction sheet, you will be asked to validate the instructions. To do so, you will affix your signature in the applicable location on the instruction sheet. The document entered above provides you with a sampling of an acknowledgement request that you may encounter during the closing process.

UNIFORM RESIDENTIAL APPRAISAL REPORT

You are advised that you have the right, under the Equal Credit Opportunity Act, to obtain a copy of your Uniform Residential Appraisal Report.

If you wish a copy, please write us at the address shown below. We must hear from you no later than 90 days after we notify you about the action taken on your credit application or you withdraw your application.

Please send your written request to:

In your letter, give the following information:

Loan or application number (if known)

Date of application

Name(s) of loan applicant(s)

Property address

Current mailing address

A copy of your Uniform Residential Appraisal Report shall be mailed to you within 30 days after receipt of your request.

Figure 11:18 Sample Appraisal Notice

When an appraisal has been conducted as a part of the transaction, the buyer has a right to obtain a copy of said appraisal if they have paid for the completion.

- If the transaction does not contain Mortgage Funding, the appraisal will often be delivered directly to the buyer or the seller.

- If the transaction has used funds from a Mortgage Lender, the appraisal will often be delivered directly to the lender during the course of the loan process.

    The Mortgage Lender will often provide instructions to the buyer on how to obtain a copy of the appraisal if they desire one.

These instructions must be signed and witnessed during the closing process.

FEE DISCLOSURE

APPLICANT(S) NAME AND ADDRESS	MORTGAGE BANKER/BROKER NAME AND ADDRESS
PROPERTY ADDRESS	TYPE OF LOAN

Today you have submitted a mortgage loan application to the Mortgage Banker or Broker listed above. All fees paid by you are nonrefundable. State law (   ) requires that the following information be disclosed to you.

The Mortgage Banker or Broker is required to refund all fees paid by an applicant borrower, other than those fees paid by the Mortgage Banker or Broker to a third party, when a mortgage loan is not produced within the time specified by the Mortgage Banker or Broker at the rate, term and overall cost agreed to by the borrower.

However, this provision shall not apply when the failure to produce a loan is due solely to the borrower's negligence, borrower's refusal to accept and close on a loan commitment or borrower's refusal or inability to provide information necessary for processing the loan, including, but not limited to, employment verifications and verifications of deposit.

This disclosure does not constitute approval of your loan or a commitment to make a loan to you.

Figure 11:19 Sample Fee Disclosure

Many lenders now require that the payment for certain fees be given to the lender by the buyer. These funds are held by the lender to pay for services that will be ordered in relationship to documenting the loan.

Other fees may be paid directly to service providers during the transaction processing stage or paid out of the proceeds at the closing table.

The lender will send disclosures directly to the buyer during the loan process, but will often request that these documents be signed again in front of the witness to the closing. The fee disclosure is one such document. The fee disclosure states that certain fees have been charged during the period leading to the closing and that if the transaction does not finalize because of an act on the part of the buyer, the buyer does not receive a refund of these fees.

KENNEY

OCCUPANCY DECLARATION

Lender:

RE: LOAN NO:
         PROPERTY ADDRESS

The undersigned Borrower of the above described property does hereby declare, under penalty of perjury as follows:

1.   Borrower shall occupy, establish and use the Property as Borrower principal residence within sixty days after execution of the Security Instrument and shall continue to occupy the Property as Borrower's principal residence for at least one year after the date of occupancy unless Lender otherwise agrees in writing, which consent shall not be unreasonably withheld, or unless extenuating circumstances exist which are beyond the Borrower's control.

      You are hereby informed that the Lender from time to time makes spot checks for owner occupancy on properties upon which we have secured a mortgage.

      Between the first and thirteenth day, after close of escrow, occupancy may be checked more than once. If after this check Lender is to believe that you never intended to occupy the subject as your primary residence, we may choose to call your note due and payable or increase your note rate by 100 basis points, in accordance with the applicable sections itemized on your note and Security Instrument and allowable by law.

2.   Borrower shall be in default, if during the loan application process, gave materially false or inaccurate information or statements to Lender (or failed to provide Lender with any material information) in connection with the loan evidenced by the Note, including but not limited to, representations concerning Borrower's occupancy of the Property as a Principal residence.

3.   The Lender has the right to foreclose on the loan under the terms of the Security Instrument if items 1 or 2 above are violated.

4.   Should Borrower's intention change prior to close transaction, then it is agreed that Lender will immediately be notified of that fact.

5.   Borrower understands that without this declaration of intention, Lender may not make the loan in connection with the property.

Figure 11:20 Sample Occupancy Declaration

When a mortgage lender provides a mortgage loan, one aspect that will affect the approval is the use that the borrower intends to make of the property for which the mortgage funds are being provided. It is commonly believed that a borrower will make payments against their primary residence better than they will against a second home, investment property or other form of residence. As such, the mortgage lender will change many aspects of the loan including interest rate, percentage of the value they will lend against and documentation requirements based on the occupancy plans of the borrower.

During the loan application process, the borrower will have provided information pertaining to the intended occupancy status of the property being transferred. You will be asked to have the borrower complete a statement that you will witness confirming these statements. This occupancy declaration will be included in nearly every closing package you complete that has mortgage funds as part of the funding figure.

You must confirm that the signatures affixed to the document are written exactly as they appear within the loan package and that the loan number and property address are correctly entered on the document.

REAL ESTATE CLOSING - SETTLEMENT AGENT

You should allow the borrower to review this document and affix their signature. You will then act as a witness confirming that the borrower is the individual who signed the document. A copy of this form must always be included within the closing package documents provided to the borrower at the end of the settlement meeting.

CERTIFICATIONS, DISCLOSURES AND NOTICES

Name(s) / Address(es) of Applicant(s):

Property Address

OCCUPANCY CERTIFICATION
The above-described applicants, as evidenced by their signatures below, certify that, upon taking (or in case of a refinance, retaining) title to the above property, their occupancy status will be:
___ Primary Residence. Occupied by owner as his / her primary residence.
___ Secondary Residence. Occupied by owner as second home, while maintaining a principal residence elsewhere.
___ Investment Property. Not owner occupied. Purchased as an investment to be held or rented.

EMPLOYMENT CERTIFICATION
Information about an applicant's employment, income, and obligations is critical to determining whether or not an application for a loan will be approved. At the time of loan closing, applicants are required to execute a sworn statement that the information supplied on the loan application about employment and income is still current, and that the applicant has not received not of, or have knowledge of an impending layoff, and that the outstanding obligations of the applicant are still substantially the same as reported on the application. If there is a change in your employment or financial circumstances prior to loan closing, you must immediately notify your loan officer in order to obtain approval of the changes.

EQUAL CREDIT OPPORTUNITY ACT
The Federal Equal Credit Opportunity Act prohibits creditors from discriminating against credit applicants on the basis of race, color, religion, national origin, sex, marital status, age (provided the applicant has the capacity to enter into a binding contract); because all or a part of the applicant's income derives from any public assistance program; or because the applicant has in good faith exercised any right under the Consumer Credit Protection Act. The federal agency that administers compliance with this law concerning this creditor is:

FAIR CREDIT REPORTING ACT
The credit standing of all individual applicants for credit will be investigated, possibly by means of a consumer report from a consumer-reporting agency. The investigative consumer report may include information about an applicant's character, general reputation, personal characteristics, and mode of living, as applicable. As an applicant, you have the right to make a written request, within a reasonable period of time, for a disclosure of the nature and scope of the investigation. If you application for credit is denied due to an unfavorable consumer report, you will be notified of the identity of the Consumer Reporting Agency which furnished the report, and of your right to request, within sixty (60) days, the reasons for the adverse actions, as required by section 615(b) of the Fair Credit Reporting Act.

ANTI-COERSION STATEMENT
The insurance laws of the State provide that the Lender may not require the Borrower to take insurance through any particular insurance agent or company to protect the mortgaged property. The Borrower, subject to the rules adopted

by the Insurance Commissioner, has the right to have the insurance placed with an Insurance Agency or Company of his or her choice, provided such Agency meets the requirements of the Lender. The Lender, however, has the right to designate reasonable financial and experience requirements as to the Company and the adequacy of the coverage.

If the selection of the Insurance Agent or Company is not mutually agreeable, then the Lender shall furnish the Borrower a copy of the Rules and Regulations promulgated by the Insurance Commissioner governing the placing of such insurance.

Applicant acknowledges having read the foregoing statement or the Rules of Insurance Commissioner relative thereto, and understands applicant's rights and privileges and those of the Lender relative to the placing of such insurance. Applicant has selected the following entities to write the insurance covering the property described above:

Insurance Company:
Agent:
Agent's Address:
Agent's Telephone Number:

GOVERNMENT LOANS ONLY
Right to Financial Privacy Act of 1978 – The Department of Housing and Urban Development and/or the Department of Veterans Affairs has the right to access financial information held by a financial institution in determining whether to qualify an applicant as a prospective mortgagor under its program requirements. Financial records regarding your transaction will be available to the Department of Housing and Urban Development and / or the Department of Veterans Affairs without further notice or authorization, but it will not be disclosed or released outside the agency except as required or permitted by law.

ACKNOWLEDGEMENT
The applicant(s) identified above certify that he/she/they have read and understand the Disclosures, Notices and Certification above, as evidenced by his/her/their signature(s) below.

Figure 11:21 Sample Certification and Disclosure

REAL ESTATE CLOSING - SETTLEMENT AGENT

Mortgage Servicing Disclosure

NOTICE TO MORTGAGE LOAN APPLICATNS: THE RIGHT TO COLLECT YOUR MORTGAGE LOAN PAYMENTS MAY BE TRANSFERRED. FEDERAL LAW GIVES YOU CERTAIN RELATED RIGHTS. READ THIS STATEMTN AND SIGN IT ONLY IF YOU UNDERSTAND ITS CONTENTS.

Because you are applying for a mortgage loan covered by the Real Estate Settlement Procedures Act (RESPA), you have certain rights under that Federal law. This statement tells you about those rights. It also tells you what the chances are that the servicing for this loan may be transferred to a different loan servicer. "Servicing" refers to collecting your principal, interest and escrow account payments, if any. If your loan servicer changes, certain procedures must be followed. This statement generally explains those procedures.

Transfer Practices and Requirements
If the servicing of your loan is assigned, sold or transferred to a new servicer you must be given notice of that transfer. The present loan servicer must send you notice in writing of the assignment, sale, or transfer of the servicing not less than 15 days before the effective date of the transfer. The present servicer and the new servicer may combine this information in one notice so long as the notice is sent to you within 15 days before the effective date of the transfer. The 15-day period is not applicable if a notice of prospective transfer is provided to you at settlement. The law allows a delay in the time (not more than 30 days after a transfer) for servicers to notify you under certain limited circumstances, when your servicer is changed abruptly. This exception applies only if your servicer is fired for cause, is in bankruptcy proceedings, or is involved in a conservatorship or receivership initiated by a Federal Agency.

Notices must contain certain information. They must contain the effective date of the transfer of the servicing of your loan to the new servicer, the name, address and toll-free or collect call telephone number of the new servicer, and toll-free or collect call telephone numbers of a person or department for both your present servicer and your new servicer to answer your questions about the transfer of servicing. During the 60-day period following the effective date of the transfer of the loan servicing, a loan payment received by your old servicer before its due date may not be treated by the new servicer as late and a late fee may not be imposed on you.

Complaint Resolution
Section 5 of RESPA gives you certain consumer rights *whether or not your loan servicing is transferred*. If you send a qualified written request to your loan servicer concerning the servicing of your loan, your servicer must provide you with a written acknowledgement within 20 business days of receipt of your request. A "qualified written request" is a written correspondence other than notice on payment coupon or other payment medium supplied by the servicer that includes your name and account number and your reasons for the request. Not later than 60 Business Days after receiving your request, your servicer must make any appropriate corrections to your account or must provide you with a written clarification regarding any dispute. During this 60-Business Day period, your servicer may not provide any information to a consumer reporting agency concerning any overdue payment related to such period or qualified written request.

A business day is any day excluding public holidays, State or Federal, Saturday or Sunday.

Damages and Costs
Section 6 of RESPA also provides for damages and costs for individuals in circumstances where servicers are shown to have violated the requirements of that section.

Servicing Transfer Estimated by Lender

1.   The following is the best estimate of what will happen to the servicing of your loan:

        We may assign, sell, or transfer the servicing of your loan sometime while the loan is outstanding. We are able to service your loan and we presently intend to service your loan.

2.   For all mortgage loans that we make in the 12-month period after your mortgage loan is funded, we estimate that the percentage of mortgage loans for which we will transfer servicing is between:

        ___ and ___%

        This is only our best estimate and it is not binding. Business conditions or other circumstances may affect

3.   This is our record of transferring the servicing of mortgage loans we have made in the past:

        Year   Percentage of Loans Transferred

ACKNOWLEDGEMENT OF MORTGAGE LOAN APPLICANT

I/We have read this disclosure form and understand the contents as evidenced by my/our signature(s) below. I/We understand that this acknowledgement is a required part of the mortgage loan application.

Figure 11:22 Sample Servicing Disclosure

NOTICE OF POSSIBLE TRANSFER OF LOAN
SERVICING ACCOUNT

Loan No.:

Borrower(s):

In the event   transfers the servicing of your loan to another Servicing Agent, you will be notified in writing by   and the new Servicing Agent.

The written information you will receive to notify you of a transfer would include:

(1)   The name and address of the Company to which the transfer of the servicing of the indebtedness is made.

(2)   The date the transfer was or will be completed.

(3)   The address where all future payments are to be made and the due date of the next payment.

I/We hereby acknowledge I/we have received and read this Notice.

Figure 11:23 Sample Servicing Disclosure 2

The servicing of a mortgage loan means the continued collection of payments, management of escrow and the handling of all post close activity relating to the mortgage loan until such time as the loan is paid in full.

Many lenders will sell the servicing rights to a mortgage to another company after the closing of the transaction. At the closing, information pertaining to how often the mortgage lender transfers servicing rights, the handling of such a transfer and the effects of such transfer on the buyer will be disclosed. It is important that the buyer understand these documents and receive a copy of all documents so that they may refer to the inclusions if, at some point, the loan servicing is transferred.

CHAPTER

12

PRO-RATA CALCULATIONS

Ongoing expenses and income will often be prorated at the time of the closing. Such proration specifics and requirements will typically be incorporated into the sales agreement. If such details are not clearly defined, then the individual who is preparing the closing package should contact the applicable parties to obtain a set of written instructions detailing what items are to be prorated and the basis to be used for such prorating.

P rorating allows for the buyer and seller to split the costs and income fairly according to the term of ownership. These prorations may be based on the date of closing or another term as negotiated within the sales contract.

Items subject to pro-rata may include

- Real estate taxes

- Homeowner's insurance premiums

- Accrued interest on assumed loans

- Rents received on income producing property

- Other income received from an income producing property

- Expenses incurred on an income producing property

- Oil or other fuel tank filling costs

- Any utility billing for any utility not turned off and paid in full prior to the date of closing

- Any other negotiated matter.

The above listing includes the most common items subject to pro rata negotiations, but as each transaction is different, the items to be prorated may be different. It is important that any financial matter that may be subject to a split between the buyer and the seller be negotiated, in writing, in the sales agreement or another document. This written negotiation ensures that all parties understand the income and expenses that may be assessed. The written negotiations also provide the settlement company with the information necessary to prorate the applicable items according to the party's wishes

30-DAY MONTH

It is customary to calculate pro-rata based on a 30-day month rather than altering pro-rata to the exact number of days within the closing month. This 30-day month is used when prorating

- Mortgage Interest

- Property Taxes

- Water Bills

- Insurance Premiums

- Other pro-rata as determined by the specific transaction

If the use of the customary 30-day month creates a significant financial impact on either the buyer or the seller, they can agree to prorate either using the exact number of days in the applicable month or to use the 365-day year to find the daily pro-rata rate.

REAL ESTATE TAXES

Real estate property tax pro-rations are common to nearly every real estate transaction. The pro-rata date calculation will depend on

- The number of times taxes are assessed per year

- The due date of each tax billing cycle

- The status of the payments of the taxes

- The period of time each payment covers

In some parts of the country, it is customary for property owners to receive and pay two sets of real estate taxes per year.

Regardless of the number of times payments are required, the method of prorating the tax payments will be the same. The only change that will occur will be that the escrow or settlement agent may be required to perform two separate sets of calculations.

To prorate taxes, you must first determine the due date of each tax payment.

- We will assume that the tax-billing period is due April 1.

You will next determine the period this billing covers.

- We will assume that the tax-billing due on April 1 is for the period of January though December 31

.The status of the payment dictates whether the seller receives tax payment reimbursement from the buyer or if the seller is required to remit tax funds for the payment of the tax billing at the time of closing.

- We will assume the tax payment was made as required by the seller on or before the due date.

Using a closing date of May 20 and the bulleted assumptions detailed above, you would perform pro-rata calculations to determine the monthly and daily tax rate using the following formula.

KENNEY

Example: Yearly Taxes $585.00   /   12   = $48.75 per month

Monthly Taxes $48.75   /   30   = $ 1.625 per day

Seller Portion January 1 though May 20

$48.75   x   4   = $195.00
$ 1.625   x   20   = $ 32.50

Total taxes assessed to seller   = $227.50

Buyer Portion May 21 through December 31

$48.75   x   7   = $341.25

$ 1.625   x   10   = $ 16.25

Total taxes assessed to buyer   = $357.50

If the tax payments are due twice yearly, you will calculate the second payment in the same manner and add both figures to achieve a total pro-rata of the taxes.

The figures will be entered as either a positive or a negative on the buyer and seller portion of the settlement statement depending on the status of the payment.

- In other words, payment for the taxes due has been made by the seller, the buyer   will repay the seller for their portion at the settlement table.

- If taxes due have not been paid by the seller, the sellers tax portion will be deducted from the funds received by the seller at the closing table.

- The taxes owing will be retained so that the billing due can be paid.

HAZARD INSURANCE

Hazard insurance is typically paid in advance based on the billing received from the hazard insurance company providing the coverage. At the beginning of each year of the policy, the premium for that year's coverage must be paid. At times, a billing cycle such as monthly or quarterly payments may be negotiated with the insurance company. When real estate is sold, the buyer may ask the seller to transfer the current insurance coverage or may obtain new coverage through the insurance company of their choice. If the existing coverage is transferred, the premiums required will be allocated to the buyer and seller respectively based upon the date of the closing or other date as negotiated in the sales contract.

The escrow or settlement agent must obtain information pertaining to the insurance coverage to begin the process of prorating the premiums. This might include

- The frequency of payment for the policy

- The total premium of the policy

- The exact term covered by the policy premium

    Example: A payment is made one time of year.

    The total premium is $660 per coverage period.

    The coverage period extends from November 1 to October 31.

    The sales contract negotiates that:

    - the buyer will assume the seller's insurance policy from the date of closing

    - closing is held on May 1

Both the buyer and the seller will be responsible for 50% of the total premium.

The seller has paid the premium in full in advance

The buyer owes the seller exactly $330 for the insurance coverage

Closings dates typically do not occur on a neat, evenly divided basis. Therefore, the pro-rata will often require more in-depth calculations than described in the above example. It is typically necessary to divide the premium coverage year into months and then divide the months into days to complete the pro-rata.

Using the previous example, suppose the closing occurred on April 30 instead of May 1. This would give the buyer 6 months and 1 day of coverage.

The first step in calculating the exact figure the buyer owes the seller is to divide the total premium into 12 monthly premium figures.

$660   /   12   = $55.00 per month

The next step is to divide the monthly premium into a daily cost basis.

$55.00   /   30   = $1.8333 per day

Next, you will multiply the monthly rate by the term the buyer will obtain

6 months   x $55.00   = $330.00

Next, you will multiply the daily rate by the daily term the buyer will obtain

1 day   x $1.8333   = $ 1.83

Total buyer premium $331.83

All figures will be rounded up or down to achieve a final figure to the nearest 1 cent.

LOAN INTEREST

When a buyer is to assume a loan from the seller, an interest pro-rata becomes necessary. Interest prorations will be handled a little differently than other prorations. Interest is typically paid in arrears. In other words, the borrower will pay interest for the use of the loan at the end of each month he has the loan. This means that if a payment is due on May 20, the monthly loan payment includes the interest due for the use of the loan principal from April 20 through May 19.

In interest pro-rata, the seller will actually owe the interest for the portion of the month the seller held the loan back to the buyer. This is a result of this arrears payment.

A closing scheduled for May 12 with the seller required to pay the interest for the date of closing, will require that the seller repay the buyer interest cost for 23 days.

April 20 – April 30	=	11 days
May 1 – May 12	=	12 days
Total interest by seller	=	23 days

Once the daily pro ratio is complete, you will calculate the daily interest figure in much the same manner as any other pro-rata.

Monthly Interest Total	$551.79	/	30 days	=	$18.393
Seller's portion	$18.393	x	23 days	=	$423.04

This figure is the portion of the interest due that the seller will be required to remit to the buyer at the closing table. This pro-rata assumes the buyer will be responsible for making the next monthly payment on the loan due following closing.

The escrow or settlement agent must pay careful attention to the sales contract when calculating pro-rata figures. If the sales agreement stipulates a different method of handling payments or pro-rata, the settlement agent must adjust their calculations accordingly.

KENNEY
RENTS AND INCOME

Prorating rents and other set forms of income sometimes takes a different form from other pro-rata you will complete. Rent and other income may be calculated using the actual number of days in the month rather than the 30-day month basis.

The seller will typically collect rents on the 1st day of the month and will therefore owe the buyer a return of the income received for the quantity of days the buyer holds the property. In other words, the payment includes all of the days from the date of closing through the end of the rental month.

At times, rents are collected on a date other than the 1st day of the month. If this is the case, you still calculate using the same methods, you simply use the rental due date as the months first day for calculation purposes.

Example: Rent due on the 7th of a 30 day month

Rent amount is $500.00

Pro-rata calculations run using the 7th to the 6th as the calendar month

Closing occurs on the 12th of the month

The seller receives the income for the date of closing

Seller receives   6 days income

500	/	30	=	$ 16.6666/daily
$16.6666	x	6	=	$100.00

Buyer receives 24 days income

500	/	30	=	$ 16.6666/daily
$16.6666	x	24	=	$400.00

Remember that the final figures are always rounded to the nearest penny to make the calculations even and to avoid discrepancies in the figures.

PRO-RATA SUMMARY

The pro-rata calculations will typically be completed using the date of the closing as the basis for the calculations, however a different date may be agreed upon by the buyer and the seller in the sales contract. If nothing is specified within the sales contract, local law and custom will dictated the pro-rata dates and methods.

Special assessments for items such as street improvements and water lines are typically not prorated. Unless specifically noted within the sales contract it is typically considered that the costs of such assessments are included within the sales price of the property and so all of the costs are allocated to the seller.

This section summarizes the most common situations in which pro-rata calculations will be completed in a real estate transaction. You should remember that this list is not all-inclusive. Any matter that must be paid or income that is received in relationship to a real estate transaction may be subject to pro-rata calculations. The handling of any additional items will be dictated by the terms of the sales contract negotiated between the buyer and the seller.

The entry of each prorated item will be included in the final settlement statement. Additional exercises are included in the exercise chapter to assist you in correctly prorating all matters. The method of inclusion for each item is covered in detail in the chapter concerning settlement statements.

CHAPTER

13

HUD 1 SETTLEMENT STATEMENT

T he settlement statement also called the HUD 1 or closing statement itemizes all of the closing costs payable at the closing or settlement meeting and details the financial negotiations of the transaction. The settlement statement provides a detailed overview of how all of the funds pertinent to the transaction are being applied.

The borrower's portion of the settlement statement should be similar to the initial Good Faith Estimate provided by the real estate agent at the time the sales contract is negotiated or by the lender at the time of the mortgage application. Additional entries or alterations may be made to the buyer's portion based upon negotiations or calculations that are more exact. The settlement statement will be considered the final authority of all transaction calculations and as such, is a very important document at the closing table.

The seller's portion of the settlement statement breaks down all items on the seller's behalf. Included in the seller's portion will be

- Any liens or mortgages that must be paid to secure a clear title to the property

- Any seller concession toward the buyer's closing costs (as negotiated in the Sales Agreement)

- Any additional charges for which the seller is responsible

- Any prorated items the seller has agreed to pay as negotiated in the sales agreement

- Any other costs the seller has incurred that must be paid at the closing table

The settlement statement contains the final figures pertaining to the loan

Page one section 100 will contain the total of all costs involved with the loan process. These will include

- The sales price

- Settlement charges

- Any pro-rated taxes due from the borrower

Section 200 will contain all amounts, which are paid on behalf of the borrower. These will include

- Any deposit or earnest money the borrower paid at the time of the Sales Agreement negotiation

- Any additional deposits or payments made by the borrower in the course of the loan processing

- The loan amount as negotiated with the lender

- Any assumed loans the borrower is taking

- Any seller financing as negotiated at the time of the sales agreement

- Any closing costs to be paid by the seller as negotiated at the time of the Sales Agreement

- Any additional adjustments that the Title Company has determined must be made to the finances of the package

The figures will be calculated, taking the amount paid on behalf of the borrower (220) and the amount due from the borrower (120) to determine the exact figure the borrower is required to bring to the closing table.

F. Type of Loan			
1__ FHA 2__ FmHA 3__ Conv 4__ VA 5__ Conv Ins	6. File Number:	7. Loan Number:	8. Mortgage Insurance Case Number

G. Note: This form is furnished to give you a statement of actual settlement costs. Amounts paid to and by the settlement agent are shown. Items marked "(P&C)" were paid outside the closing; they are shown here for informational purposes and are not included in the totals.

D. Name & Address of Borrower.	E. Name & Address of Seller	F. Name & Address of Lender
G. Property Location	H. Settlement Agent	I. Settlement Date
	Place of Settlement:	

J. Summary of Borrower's Transaction		K. Summary of Seller's Transaction	
100. Gross Amount Due From Borrower		**400. Gross Amount Due To Seller**	
101. Contract Sales Price		401. Contact Sales Price	
102. Personal Property		402. Personal Property	
103. Settlement Charges to borrower (line 1400)		403.	
104.		404.	
105.		405.	
Adjustments for items paid by seller in advance		Adjustments for items paid by seller in advance	
106. City / Town Taxes for		406. City / Town Taxes for	
107. County Taxes for		407. County Taxes for	
108. Assessments for		408. Assessments for	
109.		409.	
110.		410.	
111.		411.	
112.		412.	
120. Gross Amount Due From Borrower		**420. Gross Amount Due To Seller**	
200. Amounts Paid By Or In Behalf Of Borrower		**500. Reductions In Amount Due To Seller**	
201. Deposit or earnest money		501. Excess deposit (see instructions)	
202. Principal amount of new loan(s)		502. Settlement charges to seller (line 1400)	
203. Existing loan(s) take subject to		503. Existing loan(s) taken subject to	
204.		504. Payoff of first mortgage loan	
205.		505. Pay off of second mortgage loan	
206.		506.	
207.		507.	
208.		508.	
209.		509.	
Adjustments for items unpaid by seller		Adjustments for items unpaid by seller	
210. City / Town Taxes for		510. City / Town Taxes for	
211. County Taxes for		511. County Taxes for	
212. Assessments for		512. Assessments for	
213.		513.	
214.		514.	
215.		515.	
216.		516.	
217.		517.	
218.		518.	
219.		519.	
220. Total Paid By/For Borrower		**520. Total Reduction Amount Due Seller**	
300. Cash At Settlement From/To Borrower		**600. Cash at Settlement To/From Seller**	
301. Gross amount due from borrower (line 120)		601. Gross amount due to seller (line 420)	
302. Less amounts paid by/for borrower (line 220)	( )	602. Less reductions in amt due seller (line 520)	( )

Figure 13:1 Sample HUD Page 1

REAL ESTATE CLOSING - SETTLEMENT AGENT

The settlement agent will use the good faith estimate provided to the buyer, the real estate sales contract, any billings received in preparation for the settlement and any closing instructions received from involved parties to generate the settlement statement. A very small amount of change in the figures of the settlement statement compared to the good faith estimate received from the buyer is normal. This is due to the pro-rata calculations of exact charges. However, if the figures vary greatly from the good faith estimate, the Settlement Statement will need to be reviewed with more care to determine exactly where the error has occurred.

Page two of the settlement statement contains a more detailed breakdown of the charges included in the section titled settlement charges to borrower. The fees and costs being charges on the loan will be included in this section. These figures will mirror the good faith estimate making an error relatively simple to find.

Upon confirming that the Settlement Statement is in agreement with the Good Faith Estimate and the expected structuring of the loan, the settlement agent should inform the buyer and the seller of the final figures on the closing package. The closing can then go forward.

101 – 401	The sales price	Included in these sections will be the exact figure the buyer is paying and the seller is receiving for the property
103	Total Buyer's Settlement Charges	The total of all settlement charges included on page 2 of the form will be calculated and entered.
109 – 112	Pro-rata	The pro-rata calculations of the hazard insurance premium, utility charges or other recurring bills that are to be divided, if applicable, is entered into this section.
120	Gross Amount	The gross amount due from the buyer is tallied and entered
201	Earnest Money	The buyer is credited with the earnest money deposit made during the negotiation of the sales agreement and any additional deposits made throughout the period between the sales agreement negotiation and the closing of the loan.

	Paid From Borrowers Funds at Settlement	Paid From Seller's Funds at Settlement
700. Total Sales/Brokers commission based on price $ @ %		
Division of Commission (line 700) as follows:		
701. $ to		
702. $ to		
703 Commission paid at Settlement		
704.		
800. Items Payable in Connection with Loan		
801. Loan Origination Fee %		
802. Loan Discount %		
803. Appraisal Fee to		
804. Credit Report to		
805. Lender's Inspection Fee		
806. Mortgage Insurance Application Fee to		
807. Assumption Fee		
808.		
809.		
810.		
811.		
900. Items Required By Lender To Be Paid In Advance		
901. Interest from to @$ / day		
902. Mortgage Insurance Premium for months to		
903. Hazard Insurance Premium for years to		
904.		
905.		
1000. Reserves Deposited With Lender		
1001. Hazard Insurance months @$ per month		
1002. Mortgage Insurance months @$ per month		
1003. City Property Taxes months @$ per month		
1004. County Property Taxes months @$ per month		
1005. Annual Assessments months @$ per month		
1006. months @$ per month		
1007. months @$ per month		
1008. months @$ per month		
1100. Title Charges		
1101. Settlement or closing fee to		
1102. Abstract or title search to		
1103. Title examination to		
1104. Title insurance binder to		
1105. Document preparation to		
1106. Notary fees to		
1107. Attorney's fees to		
(includes above items numbers:)		
1108. Title Insurance to		
(includes above items numbers:)		
1109. Lender's coverage $		
1110. Owner's coverage $		
1111.		
1112.		
1113.		
1200. Government Recording and Transfer Charges		
1201. Recording fees: Deed $: Mortgage $: Releases $		
1202. City/county tax/stamps: Deed $: Mortgage $		
1203. State tax/stamps: Deed $: Mortgage $		
1204.		
1205.		
1300. Additional Settlement Charges		
1301. Survey to		
1302. Pest Inspection to		
1400. Total Settlement Charges (enter on lines 103, Section J and 502, Section K)		

Figure 13:3 Sample HUD Page 2

L. SETTLEMENT CHARGES

700   TOTAL SALES/BROKER'S COMMISSION based on price $ @   %   =

PAID FROM BORROWER'S FUNDS AT SETTLEMENT

PAID FROM SELLER'S FUNDS AT SETTLEMENT

701   Division of the commission

702   Division of the commission

703   Commission paid at Settlement

704.

800	Items Payable in Connection with Loan:	These are the fees that lenders charge to process, approve and make the mortgage loan
801	Loan Origination	This fee is usually known as a loan origination fee but sometimes is called a "point" or "points."
		It is paid to the lender.
802	Loan Discount	Also often called "points" or "discount points," a loan discount is a one-time charge imposed by the lender or broker to lower the rate at which the lender or broker would otherwise offer the loan.
803	Appraisal Fee	This charge pays for an appraisal report made by an appraiser.
805	Credit Report Fee	This fee covers the cost of a credit report.
806	Lender's Inspection Fee	This charge covers inspections, often of newly constructed housing, made by employees of the lender or by an outside inspector.
		Pest or other inspections made by companies other than the lender are discussed in line 1302.

807	Mortgage Insurance Application Fee	This fee covers the processing of an application for mortgage insurance.
808	Assumption Fee	This is a fee, which is charged when a buyer "assumes" or takes over the duty to pay the seller's existing mortgage loan.
809	Mortgage Broker Fee	Fees paid to mortgage brokers would be listed here.
900	Items Required by Lender to Be Paid in Advance:	Certain items may require payment at the time of settlement, such as accrued interest, mortgage insurance premiums and hazard insurance premiums.
901	Interest	The interest that accrues from the date of settlement to the first monthly payment.
902	Mortgage Insurance Premium	The first years mortgage insurance premium or a lump sum up-front premium.
903	Hazard Insurance Premium	Hazard insurance protects against loss due to fire, windstorm, and natural hazards.
		Lenders often require the borrower to bring to settlement a paid-up first year's policy or to pay for the first year's premium at settlement.
904	Flood Insurance	If the property requires flood insurance, the premium is usually listed here.
1000	RESERVES DEPOSITED WITH LENDER:	These lines identify the payment of taxes and/or insurance and other items that must be made at settlement to set up an escrow account.
1001	Hazard Insurance	months @ $ per month
1002	Mortgage insurance	months @ $ per month
1003.	City property taxes	months @ $ per month
1004	County property taxes	months @ $ per month

1005	Annual assessments	months @ $ per month
1006		months @ $ per month
1007		months @ $ per month
1008	Aggregate Adjustment	
1100	Title Charges:	Title charges may cover a variety of services performed by title companies and others.
1101	Settlement or Closing Fee	This fee is paid to the settlement agent or escrow holder. Responsibility for payment of this fee should be negotiated between the seller and the buyer.
1102	Abstract of Title/ Title Examination/ Binder	The charges on these lines cover the costs of the title search and examination.
1105	Document Preparation	This is a separate charged to cover the costs of preparation of final legal papers, such as a mortgage, deed of trust, note or deed.
1106	Notary Fee	This fee is charged for the cost of having a person witness the signing of the documents. The costs associated with this entry will be associated with gaining your services as the settlement agent.
1107	Attorney's Fees	The cost of any attorney appears here.
1108	Title Insurance	The total cost of owner's and lender's title insurance is shown here.
1109	Lender's Title Insurance	The cost of the lender's policy is shown here.
1115	Owner's (Buyer's) Title Insurance:	The cost of the owner's policy is shown here.
1200	Government Recording and Transfer Charges:	Transfer taxes, which in some localities are collected whenever property changes hands or a mortgage loan is made, are set by state and/or local governments.

City, county and/or state tax stamps may have to be purchased as well (lines 1202 and 1203).

1201	Recording fees	Deed $; Mortgage $; Releases $
1202	City/county tax/stamps	Deed $; Mortgage $
1203	State tax/stamps	Deed $; Mortgage $
1204		
1205		
1301	Additional Settlement Charges:	
1302	Survey	If it is required that a surveyor conduct a property survey the cost is entered here.
1303	Pest and Other Inspections	This fee is to cover inspections for termites or other pest infestation.
1304	Lead-Based Paint Inspections	This fee is to cover inspections or evaluations for lead-based paint hazard risk assessments and may be on any blank line in the 1300 series.
1400	Total Settlement Charges:	

- The sum of all fees in the borrower's column entitled "Paid from Borrower's Funds at Settlement" is placed here.

  This figure is then transferred to line 103 of Section J, "Settlement charges to borrower" in the Summary of the Borrower's Transaction on page 1 of the HUD-1 Settlement Statement. The settlement charges will then be added to the purchase price.

- The sum of all of the settlement fees paid by the seller is transferred to line 502 of Section K, Summary of Seller's Transaction on page 1 of the HUD-1 Settlement Statement.

- Paid Outside Of Closing ("POC")   Some fees may be listed on the HUD-1 to the left of the borrower's column and marked "P.O.C."

- Fees such as those for credit reports and appraisals are usually paid by the borrower before closing/settlement.

- The first page of the HUD-1 Settlement Statement summarizes all the costs and adjustments for the borrower and seller.

Section J is the summary of the borrower's transaction.

Section K is the summary of the seller's side of the transaction.

Section 100 summarizes the borrower's costs, such as the contract cost of the house, any personal property being purchased, and the total settlement charges owed by the borrower from Section L.

Beginning at line 106, adjustments are made for items (such as taxes, assessments, and fuel) that the seller has previously paid and for which the borrower will reimburse the seller.

All financial matters pertinent to the transaction will be included on the settlement statement. All parties will sign the statement to confirm that they understand and agree with the inclusions.

Title Company Disclosure Form

Title Company File No.

RE:
Property Address:

This, the day _____ of _____, 20___, came _____known as
Borrower/Buyer and_____Seller (fill in Seller's name, if this is a Sale of the
Property), and acknowledged receipt and disclosure of the following items. Said party(s) also acknowledge that ____
_____ in and for the State of _____ ("know collectively as
"COMPANY" or "TITLE COMPANY") is relying on the foregoing, and without such acknowledgement, the said
COMPANY would not issue its Policy(s) of Title Insurance.

INSTRUCTIONS for completing this form:
If this is a Refinance, Borrower INITIAL 3s 1, 3a, 5, 6, 7, 8, 10, and 11
If this is a Purchase, both Borrower and Seller to INITIAL where appropriate.

Figure 13:3 Sample Title Company Disclosure Page 1

Seller's Initials	Borrower's Initials	1.) AFFIDAVIT OF DEBTS AND LIENS. Borrower and Seller each acknowledge that there are no other liens, judgments or other involuntary liens served, filed or recorded against said parties, and that effect the Real Property, that is not already disclosed, the parties swear and/or affirm the following as current liens or judgments effecting the real property. (if none, write "none"):
	Borrower's Initials	2.) WAIVER OF INCPECTION. Since examines only the record title and does not actually see the property, we hereby waive inspection by of this property and accept our policy subject to the rights of parties in possession. We agree that it is our responsibility to inspect said premises and to obtain possession of it from the present occupants, if any.
Seller's Initials	Borrower's Initials	3. (A) ACCPETANCE OF SURVEY. Borrower has received and reviewed a copy of the survey, if any, of the Property made in connection with this transaction and acknowledges being aware of the following matters of encroachment, protrusion, conflict, or discrepancy disclosed by the survey. If there is no survey, you affirm that there have been no changes to the property since the day of the last survey that would trigger encroachments or protrusions over dedicated easements or building setback lines. If you do not know the answer to this question, write on the spaces below, any improvements to the property, e.g. swimming pools, additions to the home, gazebos or other structures, whether temporary or permanent that are not won the property since you became Owner. DO NOT indicate new Landscaping. NOTE ALOS: That the transaction may involve NEW CONSTRUCTION, for which no survey is yet prepared at the time of closing. The Borrower's herein acknowledge they are responsible to provide a FINAL SURVEY to the "Company" after completion and acceptance of the construction. Any final Policy of Title Insurance will be subject to those matters shown within such FINAL SURVEY.
	Borrower's Initials	3. (B) BOUNDARY COVERAGE. As proposed to be issued, Borrower's Owner Policy will contain a general exception to any discrepancies or conflicts in area or Boundary lines, and any encroachments, protrusions, or overlapping of improvements. ON payment of an additional Owners Policy premium, policy coverage against these matters is available subject to TITLE COMPANY'S approval of a current survey of the Property and without limiting specific exceptions to matters disclosed by the survey. If you want the additional coverage and this is a Purchase, so indicate by writing YES:
Seller's Initials	Borrower's Initials	4.) PROPERTY TAX PRORATIONS. Property taxes for the current year have been prorated between BUYER and SELLER, who each acknowledge and understand that these prorations are based upon (a) the sales price or the most current appraised value available and the most current tax rate available or (b) some other common method of estimation. SELLER warrants and represents that there are no past due taxes owed on the Property and if such warranty and representation is untrue the SELLER shall reimburse the Title Company, on demand, for any sums paid by the Title Company to pay such taxes, and any related penalty and interest. BUYER and SELLER each agree that when amounts of the current year's taxes become known and payable they will adjust any changes of the proration and reimbursement between themselves and that TITLE COMPANY shall have no liability or obligation with respect to these prorations.

Figure 13:4 Sample Title Company Disclosure Page 2

	Borrower's Initials	5.) TAX RENDITION AND EXEMPTIONS. Although the Central Appraiser District (CAD) may independently determine Borrower's new ownership and billing address, BUYER is still obligated by law to "render" the Property for taxation by notifying the CAD of the changes in the Property's ownership and of BORROWER'S proper address for tax billing. BUYER is advised that current year's taxes may have been assessed on the basis of various exemptions obtained by SELLER (e.g., homestead or over 65). It is the BORROWER'S responsibility to qualify for BORROWER'S own tax exemptions and to meet any requirements prescribed by the taxing authorities. BUYER Acknowledges and understands these obligations and the fact that TITLE COMPANY assumes no responsibility for accuracy of CAD records concerning ownership, tax-billing address, or status of exemptions.
	Borrower's Initials	6.) HOMEOWNER'S ASSOCIATION. Buyer acknowledges that ownership of the PROPERTY involves membership in a homeowner's association. BORROWER is responsible for contacting the homeowner's association immediate to asce3rtain the exact amount of future dues or assessments. TITLE COMPANY has made no representations with respect to, such Association's annual budget, pending repairs or deferred maintenance, if any, or other debts of the association. BUYER accepts sole responsibility to obtain such information and verify its accuracy to BORROWER'S satisfaction. IF THERE IS NO HOMEOWNER'S ASSOCIATION – PLEASE DISREGARD.
Seller's Initials	Borrower's Initials	7.) CLOSING DISCLAIMER. SELLER and BORROWER ach acknowledge and understand that the above referenced transaction has not yet "closed". Any change in possession of the Property takes place AT BORROWER'S AND SELLER'S OWN RISK. THIS TRANSACTION IS NOT CLOSED UNTIL: A) ALL TITLE REQUIREMENTS ARE COMPLETED TO THE SATISFACTION OF TITLE COMPANY. B) ALL NECESSARY DOCUMETNS ARE PROPERLY EXECUTED, REVIEWED, AND ACCPETED BY THE PATRIES TO THIS TRANSACTION AND BY TITLE COMPANY; AND, C) ALL FUNDS ARE COLLECTED AND DELIVERED TO AND ACCEPTED BY THE PARTEIS TO WHOM THEY ARE DUE.
	Borrower's Initials	8.) ARBITRATION. Depending on the language of our Title Policy in your State, we may arbitrate any title disputes.
Seller's Initials		9.) IRS REPORTING. SELLER acknowledges having received at closing a copy of the HUD-1 Settlement Statement as a Substitute Form 1099-8. In accordance with federal tax regulations, information from the HUD-1 Statement will be furnished to the Internal Revenue Service.
Seller's Initials	Borrower's Initials	10.) ERRORS AND OMMISSIONS. In the event that any of the documents prepared in connection with the closing of this transaction contain errors which misstate or inaccurately reflect the true and correct terms, conditions and provisions of this closing, and the inaccuracy or misstatement is due to a clerical error or to a unilateral mistake on the part of the TITLE COMPANY, or to a mutual mistake on the part of the TITEL COMPANY AND/OR THE SELLER AND/OR THE BUYER, the undersigned agree to execute, in a timely manner, such correction documents as TITLE COMPANY may deem necessary to remedy such inaccuracy or misstatement.

Figure 13:4 Sample Title Company Disclosure Page 3

	Borrower's Initials	11.) ATTORENY REPRESENTATION NOTICE. BUYER may wish to consult an attorney to discuss the matters shown on Schedule B or C of the Commitment for Title Insurance that was issued in connection with this transaction. The Title Insurance Policy will be a legal contract between BUYER and the underwriter. Neither the Commitment for Title Insurance nor the Title Insurance Policy are abstracts of title, title reports, or representations of title. They are contracts of indemnity. No representation is made that your intended use of the Property is allowed under law or under the restrictions or exceptions affecting the Property.

Figure 13:4 Sample Title Company Disclosure Page 4

The title company who has issued the applicable documents for the transaction you are closing will often request that you have the buyer and seller involved in a transaction complete a disclosure notice. This disclosure notice details specific parameters under which the title company is issuing title insurance and other applicable transaction details.

The specific subsections of the document must be initials by the party affected by each section. In other words, some sections will require the initials of the buyer, other sections will require the seller initial the document and some sections will require the initials of both parties to the transaction. It is very important that the applicable party review each section and place their initials in the appropriate locations. You will want to review the document prior to the final affixation of signatures to ensure that all sections have been duly accepted by the applicable party.

After all initials have been affixed in the appropriate location, the buyer and the seller will affix their signature to the document. It is important that you confirm that the signatures appear exactly as they have been typed.

You will witness each signature and affix your notary seal to the document.

RE: Escrow No.

PROCEEDS AUTHORIZTION

Buyer(s):

Property Address:

1.   One check payable to _____

      Mailed to this address_____

      _____

      a.   Regular Mail
      b.   Overnight Mail
      c.   Overnight Mail with Release Signature

2.   Wired to this account (I understand there is a $15 Fee)

      ABA Routing No._____

      Bank Name _____

      Name on Account _____

      Account No. _____

Figure 13:5 Sample Proceeds Authorization

CHAPTER
14

SIGNING AND POST CLOSE

Each closing that you oversee will have unique instructions that you must follow. *These instructions will vary greatly from transaction to transaction but will always contain some of the key components as the samples that we have included for your review. Each series of closing instructions result from the specifics of all of the tasks and processes that led to the closing. They will be generated using pertinent information from the sales agreement, addendums, contingencies, title report, financing conditions and any other matter that occurred during the preparatory phase of the real estate transfer. The closing instructions you will receive are essentially a detailing of the exact steps you must take to finalize the closing.*

Your closing instructions will often begin with a statement such as

> *"You are hereby authorized and directed to do the following..."*

You could be you as the settlement agent, the title company or a combination of the two.

The closing instructions will specify the various conditions and tasks that must be completed at the actual settlement to finish the closing process and legally transfer the ownership of the subject property to the new buyer. The instructions will detail every item relating to the transaction. Some common inclusions to the instructions include

- who will pay for what items

- exact signatures that are required

- where signatures must be placed

- any items that the buyer or the seller is required to provide to you for copy at the closing table

- A listing of documents that must be signed and by whom

- A listing of documents or items that must be remitted and by whom such as proof of homeowners insurance or a satisfactory termite report

- A detail of what money each individual must bring to the closing table.

- A listing of what billings must be paid in relationship to the transaction

- Conditions that must be met prior to close including the completion of mortgage documents, releases and any other matter that has not been finalized during the period leading to closing

- A listing of specific items to be prorated and how the pro-rata will be applied

- An explanation of all fees that are entered on the settlement statement for either the buyer or the seller

- Instructions will often end with an authorization to disperse funds to the parties owed money in the transaction

Each transaction is different and thus the closing instructions for each transaction will be different. The items listed above will be common to may of the transactions you will close and the closing package samples included within this program will provide you with examples of the most common documents you will encounter.

If you receive closing instructions that contain an item that you have not encountered before or on which you are unclear, you should contact the company or individual who generated the instructions to be certain that you complete all required tasks prior to finalizing the meeting and allowing the parties to leave.

It is suggested that you take time to review every closing package that you receive prior to arriving at the settlement meeting. This review will allow you to determine if there are any unusual or confusing instructions contained within the listing and to obtain clarification or enhanced instruction for those unusual items you have not encountered in the past.

POST CLOSE

After all of the closing conditions have been satisfied, the applicable documents have been signed and notarized, and the buyer and seller have left the settlement meeting, additional post-close tasks must be accomplished before the transaction can be considered complete.

Whether the completion of all, some or none of these post close tasks falls under your job descriptions or that of another individual will depend on the company for which you work. It is important that you understand the functions that must occur following the signing of the documents to finalize the transaction. This understanding will enable you to express the next steps in the process and set the expectations of the buyer and the seller as to when all of the transaction requirements will be satisfied. This is especially important from the perspective of the seller in that funds are often not dispersed until all post close actions are completed.

After all of the applicable closing documents have been signed, one of the first post close tasks will be to provide the documents to the lender in compliance with their requirements. Receipt of these fully endorsed documents if often the last step in gaining the order to release the transaction funds. Many lenders actually require the entire closing package to be in their hands before they are willing to fund the loan.

Once the lender has funded the loan and all buyer or seller payments are in the hands of the closing company the next step is to issue the applicable closing checks. These checks will be written to pay off any bills in relationship to the transaction. These might include

- mortgage loans or liens for which the seller is responsible

- the seller's portion of the purchase proceeds

- any billings that are linked to the transaction such as appraisal fees or inspection costs

- any commission due to the real estate agents

- any other matter that is listed on the instructions or for which an agreed upon bill has been presented during the period leading to the close

The agent for the closing who is responsible for recording documents will then take all applicable items to the courthouse for recording in the public records system. This is an important task in that it provides public knowledge of the transfer of ownership and will be reviewed in future public records searches.

- This public recordation provides security to the buyer, lender and seller because it makes public all records of the transaction.

- This recordation in the county recorders office is known as constructive notice and is the means used to prove ownership of a property.

CERTIFICATE OF RECORDATION OF DOCUMENTS

LENDER:

The undersigned hereby certifies that all documents that necessitate recordation in connection with that certain loan made by the above Lender to

Mortgagor, have been sent for recording to the Office of the Clerk of the Circuit Court of the county or city wherein the property lies.

Executed this day of:

Figure 14:1 Sample Certificate of Recordation

The individual responsible for completing the recording tasks will often endorse a certification of recordation. This document will become a part of the transaction file and will enable anyone who reviews the file to see who completed the recording functions. The certification of recordation will also be sent to the mortgage lender as proof that the final, legal notices have been completed.

Following the recording of all applicable documents, the purchase or transfer of the real property is considered officially closed. When the transaction is officially closed, all funds are released and your functions as the settlement agent are at an end.

CHAPTER
15

RESPA

Real Estate Settlement Procedures Act (RESPA)

The Real Estate Settlement Procedures Act (RESPA) is enforced by HUD and deals with closing costs and settlement procedures. The purpose of RESPA is to regulate the processes of closing practices across the United States. RESPA prohibits specific practices in relationship to the transfer of property that involves a first mortgage loan on a one to four unit dwellings.

The purposes of RESPA are to:

- Help consumers in shopping for settlement services.

- Eliminate referral fees that increase the costs of certain settlement services.

RESPA requires that borrowers receive disclosures at various times during the mortgage application and home purchase processes.

RESPA prohibits a person from giving or accepting any thing of value for referrals of settlement service business.

RESPA prohibits a person from giving or accepting any part of a charge for services that are not performed.

RESPA prohibits home sellers from requiring homebuyers to purchase title insurance from a particular company.

RESPA restricts the amount of property tax and insurance payments that may be paid in advance at or prior to the closing.

> The amount is limited to the owner's share of the taxes and insurance that is due at the time of settlement plus $1/6^{th}$ of the amount that will become due for these items within the 12-month period following settlement.

The Federal Government as well as most State Governing bodies have established laws and acts that you will use to create the policies and procedures with which you handle each potential closing and business contact.

These laws are in place to protect the interest of the public and to make the obtainment of housing and home mortgage funds a fair practice for all applicants. You must incorporate the required practices into your daily task list to ensure you handle each closing task in compliance with the RESPA requirements.

You are entering a professional career much like that of a physician or attorney and you must ensure that your behavior and actions are above reproach.

Settlement Agent Basic Training
Expanded Course Guide

Introduction

Title Closing — 1

Chapter 1

Types of Meetings — 4

Chapter 2

Party Obligations — 8
Seller's Responsibility — 8
Buyers Responsibility — 9
Escrow Agent — 10
Sample Timetable — 11

Chapter 3

Meeting Overview — 12
Round Table Meeting — 13
Escrow — 15

Chapter 4

Opening Escrow — 19
Sample Escrow Form — 21

Chapter 5

Potential Delays — 22

Chapter 6

The sales contract — 24
Sample Contract — 26
Contract Inclusions — 27

Chapter 7

The Title Search — 47
Title Commitment and Insurance — 49

Chapter 8

Deeds — 51
Types of Deeds — 52
Sample General Warranty Deed — 58
Form and Inclusions of Deeds — 60
Warranties of Title — 62
Limitations in the Deed — 64

Sample Tax Deed — 66
Sample Quitclaim Deed — 68

Chapter 9

How Title Is Held — 69
Signature Requirements — 70
Ownership Methodology — 70
Types of Unity — 71
Types of Tenancy — 71
Sample Tenancy Change Form — 73

Chapter 10

Loan Commitment and Security — 74
Closing Instructions — 75
Note — 78
Components of a Note — 79
Sample Note Addendum — 81
Mailing Address Confirmation — 82
Mortgage Documents — 84
Mortgage Key — 85
Mortgage Covenants — 86
Mortgage Assumption — 88
Sample Assumption Addendum — 89
Sample Assumption Agreement — 91

Chapter 11

Verifications and Certifications — 94
Itemization Amount Financed — 95
Correction Agreement — 96
Warranty and Compliance — 97
Tax Certificate — 98
Impound/Non Impound Notice — 99
TIL — 100
Contact Information Request — 102
Credit Bureau Notice — 103
General Authorization — 104
Identity Verification / Acknowledgement — 105
Terrorism Notice — 107
Signature Affidavit/ AKA Statement — 108
Closing Validation — 109
Appraisal Notice — 110
Fee Disclosure — 111
Occupancy Declaration — 112
Certification, Disclosures, Notices Form — 113

Servicing Disclosure   115

Chapter 12

Pro-Rata Calculations   117

30-Day Month   118

Real Estate Taxes   119

Hazard Insurance   121

Loan Interest   123

Rents and Income   124

Pro-Rata Summary   125

Chapter 13

HUD 1 Settlement Statement   126

Sample Statement   128

Inclusion Explanation   129

Title Company Disclosure   135

Proceeds Authorization   139

Chapter 14

Signing and Post Close   140

Instructions   140

Post Close   142

Certificate of Recordation   143

Chapter 15

RESPA   144

Appendix A Expanded Course Guide   147

Appendix B Glossary of Terms   149

Appendix C Study Guide   153

APPENDIX B
GLOSSARY OF TERMS

Abstract of Title: the chronological history of the most relevant parts of every recorded instrument regarding a title

Abstractor: individual who specializes in research relevant to the chain of title

Abut: touch

Accretion: the build-up of soil caused by the action of water or wind

Accrue: to increase or accumulate. Mortgage interest is said to accrue daily

Acknowledgement: a declaration made before a notary or other official certifying that the signing of a document is of a voluntary act undertaken of ones own free will

Actual Notice: personal knowledge of an interest or instrument

Addendum: an attachment to a purchase agreement or to escrow instructions that alters or negotiates the transaction specifics

Ad Valorem: a Latin term that means 'according to value' Taxes are sometimes assessed on an ad valorem basis

Adverse Possession: obtaining title from another by the open, hostile, continuous use of property for a specific period set forth by statute

Affidavit: a statement sworn under oath or before a notary

Affirmation: a formal declaration regarding the truthfulness of a statement

Affirmative Easement: a type of easement that allows the easement holder the right to use the land of another landowner

Agreement of Sale: the real estate purchase contract

Air Rights: the rights to the use of the airspace located above a piece of property

Alienation Clause: a clause that calls an entire loan balance due and payable This is also termed an acceleration clause or due on sale clause

Allodial System: a system of land ownership where the ownership is held by individuals rather than the government The US follows this system of ownership

Alluvion: the gradual addition of soil to a property by the action of water

Amendment: A change made to correct an error or to alter an agreement.

Amortization: The method by which a loan is paid down with each subsequent payment

Annual Percentage Rate: the yearly rate of interest on a loan

Antenuptial Agreement: an agreement executed between a man and a woman prior to marriage to resolve and settle future issues

Appropriation Process: The enactment of a taxing authority's budget and money sources into legally required payment.

Appurtenance: rights, benefits and attachments that transfer with real property

Appurtenant Easement: an easement that transfers with the land

Arrears: term used when describing a past due payment

ARM: adjustable rate mortgage

Assessed Value: the value placed on a property by the county assessor

Assessor's Map: The map that shows the assessor's parcel number for all land parcels within a specific taxing area

Assignment: the transfer, in writing, of one's interest in something

Assumption: the taking over of another person's financial obligation

Balloon Payment: the final payment that pays a note in full

Bankruptcy: a legal procedure that eliminates unsecured debt or relinquishes property to eliminate secured debt

Bargain and Sale Deed: a deed that uses the term bargain and sale and contains no warranties other than implied interest on the part of the seller

Base Line: Latitude line that acts as a reference in the rectangular survey system

Bilateral Escrow Instructions: a set of escrow instructions signed by both the buyer and the seller

Binder: insurance coverage given by an agent prior to the issuance of the full insurance policy

Bundle of Rights: all rights of ownership of real property. Synonym for estate

Certificate of Title: evidence of title issued by a registrar

Cession Deed: deed that conveys all rights of an individual in real property to a county or municipality

Chain of Title : the history, in chronological order, of a property from the original government grant to the present owner

Close of Escrow: the date when the documents are recorded and title passes from the seller to the buyer

Closing Costs: the costs that are payable to close escrow not including the purchase price of a property

Cloud on Title: a claim, document, defect or discrepancy that casts doubt on the marketability of a title

Collateral: real or personal property pledged as security for a loan

Commitment of Title: the guarantee from a title company that they will provide title insurance Also termed a preliminary title report

Competent: legally qualified to conduct transactions

Concurrent Escrow: a procedure where the one closing is dependent on the completion of another closing Also termed a double escrow

Condemnation: the legal action to take a property for public use by eminent domain

Consideration: the amount of money or services given in exchange for the transfer of a property

Constructive Notice: the notice given by occupancy or recording of an interest in real property

Contingency: a condition that must be met or event that must happen before a contract will be considered binding

Convey: the transfer of title from one person to another

Covenant: a written agreement as to the use of a property

Declaration of Restriction: declaration of the restrictions contained in a deed of conveyance

Deed: a document that conveys interest and title to real property

Deed in Lieu of Foreclosure: a deed from a property owner to a lien holder made to avoid full foreclosure proceedings.

Deemer Period: the method that the state regulates the rate of filing by the title company

Deficiency Judgment: a judgment obtained when the foreclosure sale does not satisfy a debt in full

Descent: the hereditary succession by law when a property owner dies without a valid will

Determinable Fee Estate: an estate that would end on the occurrence of a specific event

Dominant Estate: an estate for which an easement is granted

Disbursement : the release of funds held in an escrow account

Earnest Money: a deposit by a buyer to a seller to bind an agreement

Easement: the right of a person to use the land of another

Easement by Necessity: an easement granted out of a valid need for the easement

Easement by Prescription: an easement created by the open, continuous, hostile and notorious use of the property of another for a specified period of time

Easement in Gross: a personal easement to use the land of another in which no dominant estate exists

Emblements: cultivated crops that are considered personal property

Eminent Domain: the government's right to take private property for public use with just compensation paid to the property owner for the loss

Encroachment: the unauthorized intrusion on, over or under the land of another

Encumbrance : any item that affects the title to real property such as liens, easements or deed restrictions

Endorsement: an addition that either expands or limits the standard coverage's provided under a title insurance policy

Escrow: the act of depositing papers and or money with an impartial third party until a transaction is complete

Escrow Instructions: a series of instructions from a buyer, seller, lender or other interested party as to the acts that must be completed and conditions that must be met prior to the transfer of a property

Equitable Title: title obtained during the period between the creation of an agreement or contract and the finalization of a transaction

Escheat: the reversion of a property to the state when a person dies without a valid will and no heirs as identified by statute

Exception in Deed: exclusion in a deed that deeds only one portion of a property

Execute to validate a document

Fee Simple Estate: the highest level of ownership possible the fee simple ownership includes the full bundle of rights

Fee Simple Determinable: a grant that ends if a property is not longer used for a designated purpose

Fee Tail Estate: an estate that limits conveyance to the heirs and decedents of the owner

Fixture: an item of personal property that is permanently attached to real property in a manner that causes it to become real property

Foreclosure: a legal process that deprives an owner of his or her rights to a property

Funding: the release of loan money from a lender to the escrow company

General Warranty Deed: a deed where the grantor warrants title against the claims of all others

Gift Deed: a deed that transfers real property for love and affection rather than valuable consideration

Good Consideration: love and affection are considered good consideration

Grant: the act of conveying title to a property

Grantee: the person who receives a deed, grant or other item

REAL ESTATE CLOSING - SETTLEMENT AGENT

Granting Clause: a deed provision showing that title is passing

Grantor: the person giving or conveying the deed, grant or other item

Grantor/Grantee Index: an index system for researching chain of title that lists grantor/grantee names

Guardianship : the administration of the property of a minor or incompetent person

Habendum: a to have and to hold clause indicating the extent of the ownership being transferred

Impound: to accumulate borrower funds to meet the periodic payments due under tax billings or insurance billings

Improvement: an addition to land that is considered real property

Indemnity: a guarantee against loss

Incompetent: a person who is deemed incapable of making a legal decision or entering a legal contract due to age or mental capacity

Informal Reference: a description of property that uses items such as number, street or address This is not a legal description of property

Instrument: a written legal document such as a sales agreement, contract or promissory note

Inverse Condemnation: an action instituted by a property owner forcing the government to take property where the property use is restricted by an action taken by the government or other public entity

Involuntary Lien: a lien imposed without the consent of a property owner

Joint Tenancy: an undivided interest that contains all unities except the unity of person

Judgment: the order by a court as to money owed or other definitive decisions

Judgment in Personam: a judgment against a person. When recorded the judgment becomes a specific lien against a particular property of the person involved in the action

Judgment in Rem: a judgment against specific property When recorded the judgment becomes a specific lien against the property involved in the action

Judicial Foreclosure: a foreclosure that requires court proceedings for finalization

Jurat: the statement or certificate of the individual witnessing signatures to specific instruments

Legal Access: the legal right to use a specified access point

Legal Description: a description of real property that can be considered legally binding

Lender Instructions: the instructions received from a lender stating the requirements that must be met before a transaction can be closed

Lien: a monetary encumbrance secured by real property

Life Estate: an estate that exists for the lifetime of a specific person

Lis Pendens: pending lawsuit

Littoral rights: the rights of a property owner to the use of a lake, pond or ocean water that borders his or her property in a reasonable manner

Marketable Title: a title that is clear of liens, encumbrances and other defects

Mechanic's Lien: a specific lien against real property placed by a contractor for work performed to the property or property improvements when the charges are not paid as agreed by the property owner

Meridians: north-south lines used by government surveyors for measuring and describing real property

Metes and Bounds: a method of legal description by measurement and boundary of real property

Monument: a fixed marker used in surveys within the metes and bounds method

Mutual Consent: approval of both parties regarding the terms of a contract

Negotiable: able to be assigned or transferred

Notary Public: the person enabled by the property authorities to witness signatures, oaths or other matters

Offset Statement: the statement by an owner or lien holder detailing the liens against a piece of property

Option: a right given by the owner of property to another to buy a property at an agreed upon price and within an agreed upon time

Personal Property: property that is not classified as real property

Physical Access: access is the actual ability to use an access point

Police Power: the power of the state to enforce laws to promote the health and safety of the general public through the taking of a privately held piece of land

Post-nuptial Agreement: an agreement executed between a husband and wife following marriage to determine and settle specific issues

Preliminary Title Report: a report indicating the present condition of the title based on items discovered during a record search

Prescription: an easement obtained by the open, hostile, continuous and notorious use of another's property for a regulated period of time

Prior Appropriation: a theory used in some states that allows the first user to divert water to maintain that sole interest in the water even though the use may not be equitable to other landowners

Priority: taking place in order or precedence over. In a real estate transaction, priority is typically established by the date of the recording of an instrument or specific wording within an instrument. Priority may be usurped by the government right of taxation

Proration: the method employed to divide taxes, interest and other sums between a buyer and a seller based upon a certain date

Quiet Enjoyment: the right of an owner to use their property without interference

Quiet Title: a court action to obtain a determination regarding ownership right

Quitclaim Deed: a deed conveying whatever interest a grantor holds in real property. This type of deed makes no claim to actual ownership

Real Property: land and all that goes with the land

Recordation: the act of recording valid documents with the office of record to serve notice to all regarding the instruments recorded

Redemption: the act of reclaiming the title to property from someone who has taken legal interest in it

Redemption Period: the time in which an individual may redeem the interest in his or her property

Release: the relinquishment or giving up of a specific right or claim of interest

Remainder Interest: an interest obtained by a third party after the expiration of a life estate

Reservation: a specific right withheld by the grantor when conveying property

Restrictive Covenant: a restriction where the owner is limited as to the use of his or her property

Reversionary Interest: an interest to a property by the original grantor following the occurrence of a specific event

Right of Way: the right to pass over the land of another

Riparian Rights: rights of a landowner to use flowing water located on, under or adjacent to his or her property in a reasonable manner

Security: the property pledged to secure the repayment of a loan

Servient Estate: an estate that bears the burden of an easement

Settlement: the time at which a property transfer is finalized

Sheriff's Deed: a deed given by a sheriff when a property is sold for the execution of a judgment or at foreclosure sale

Special Warranty Deed: a deed where the seller warrants the title only against defects occurring during his or her ownership

Specific Lien: a lien against a particular piece of property

Statute of Limitations: the time limit within which legal proceedings may be implemented and action brought

Subject To: to take title without paying off one or more existing liens or notes

Sub-surface Rights: the right to the space and natural resources contained below the surface of a particular parcel of land

Surface Rights: the right to use the surface of a parcel of land. Commonly known as the rights to the land and the improvements of the land

Survey : a verification of property lines or the creation of a legal description created by a surveyor

Survivorship: the right of a joint tenant to obtain the interest of another tenant upon the death of the other party or other event that negates the interest of the other party

Tax Deed: a deed obtained as a result of a tax sale

Tenancy: method of holding ownership or interest in a property

Tenancy by the Entirety: a form of joint tenancy held by husband and wives and containing all of the forms of unity

Tenancy in Common: a form of joint tenancy by two or more individuals or entities where each obtains an undivided interest in real property

Title: ownership Title is passed by deed

Title Insurance: the insurance policy that agrees to indemnify the insured against defects in the title

Vendee: buyer

Vendor: seller

Vest: to convey or confer

Vesting: the manner in which title to real property is held. Method of interest in real property

Void: having no legal effect

Voidable: capable of being voided or valid only until voided

Voluntary Lien: a lien created by the action of the property owner in consideration of money borrowed

Waiver: the release of a right

REAL ESTATE SETTLEMENT APPENDIX C

Study Workbook

1.   Title Closing is the time when a real estate transaction?

_____

_____

_____

_____

2.   Other common terms used to describe title include:

_____

_____

_____

3.   What common forms of funds may the borrower bring to the closing?

_____

_____

_____

_____

4.   It is the function of the settlement agent to?

_____

_____

_____

_____

5.   Prorating is:

_____

_____

_____

_____

Chapter 1 – Types of Meetings

1.   It is a critical portion of your function at the meeting to _____ that all necessary _____ _____ are obtained and to _____ these _____.

2.   During the closing, all matters negotiated in the sales agreement will be _____ and confirmation that all _____ have been met will be made by both the buyer and the seller.

3.   The escrow agents task list should detail every _____, _____, and applicable _____ that must occur to reach the final legal _____ f the property.

4.   If the buyer or seller is unable to attend the closing or another individual expected to attend is unable to be present, a _____ will be _____.

5.   The parties to a transaction are _____ likely to meet if the closing is completed in the form of an _____ _____.

6.   The most common forms of settlement are the

_____

_____

_____

_____

_____

7.   What is the primary component that defines a round table closing?

_____

_____

_____

_____

_____

8.   When you are proving settlement services for a transaction that contains a mortgage, the lender will often provide

_____

_____

_____

_____

9.   A transaction cannot be considered finalized until

_____

_____

_____

_____

10.   What is a power of attorney?

_____

_____

_____

_____

_____

11.   A round table closing dictates that all parties

_____

_____

_____

_____

_____

Chapter 2 – Party Obligations

1.   The escrow agent will use the _____ as a _____ to the
tasks that must be completed in order for the transaction to close.

2.   Escrow or settlement processes can typically be completed in _____.

3.   What are the three most common items the seller or seller's attorney is responsible for providing at the closing
meeting?

_____

_____

_____

_____

_____

4.   The buyer is responsible for having

_____

_____

_____

_____

5.   The lender will provide

_____

_____

_____

_____

6.   What are the three most common items the lender will provide for a closing that uses mortgage funds?

_____

_____

_____

_____

7.   Name the three most common tasks an escrow agent must complete at the closing table?

_____

_____

_____

_____

_____

8   An offset statement is

_____

_____

_____

_____

_____

9.   Prior to closing the settlement agent should contact each party and confirm

_____

_____

_____

_____

_____

10.   What are the most common tasks the settlement agent will perform at and immediately following the settlement meeting?

_____

_____

_____

_____

_____

Chapter 3 – Meeting Overviews

1. A representative may have been _____ by one of the parties to _____ on their behalf at the settlement meeting.

2. The settlement agent will _____ the _____ of all parties present at the meeting.

3. The escrow agent is a _____ third party selected by the _____ and the _____ _____.

4. Most States require that the settlement agent obtain a _____ copy of _____ for each party who will be signing documents.

5. The mortgage lender will provide _____ of the required _____ and _____ that must be completed to secure the mortgage loan on the _____

6. If an existing loan is to be assumed by the buyer as part of the transaction, the escrow agent will obtain the ____ _____ _____ _____ and any . _____ required by the buyer or the seller to complete the _____ .

7. The settlement may also be termed

_____

_____

_____

_____

_____

8. At a dry closing, the fund from the lender

_____

_____

_____

_____

_____

9. When will the funds from a dry closing be provided to the settlement agent?

_____

_____

_____

_____

_____

10. What is included in the escrow instructions?

_____

_____

_____

_____

_____

Chapter 4 – Opening Escrow

1.	Commissions are _____ to be paid to _____ _____ and must be noted at the opening of escrow and incorporated into the settlement statement.

2.	The _____ _____ will detail the specifics of any mortgages that must be _ _____ prior to the transfer of the property.

3.	The escrow agent will generate a transaction timeline based on the _____ _____ detailed in the _____

4.	The firs task upon receipt of a new closing order is to

_____

_____

_____

_____

_____

5.	Name the five most common items that the closing agent should note when a new closing order is received:

_____

_____

_____

_____

_____

6.	The financial specifics of a transaction of interest to the closing agent will include

_____

_____

_____

_____

_____

REAL ESTATE CLOSING - SETTLEMENT AGENT

7.   If a real estate agent is involved in the transaction, the two essential pieces of interest to the closing agent are

_____

_____

_____

_____

_____

8.   The settlement agent will review the sales agreement to confirm

_____

_____

_____

9.   Name the four most common parties that must review and approve property inspections before the closing can commence

_____

_____

_____

_____

10.   The closing agent must obtain legal verification of

_____

_____

_____

_____

Chapter 5 – Potential Delays

1.   The expected _____ for a real estate transaction will typically be included on the ____
        _____.

2.   If it becomes apparent that the agreed upon close date will not be met, an _____ to the __
        _____ must be created that _____
        the closing date.

3.   If a contract cancellation occurs, the settlement agent must determine if there are _____
        _____ outstanding and have the _____ who is deemed _____
        _____ for the cancellation or is detailed as the responsible party within the contracts make
        payment.

4.   The functions of the settlement agent will often be the _____ items requiring _____
        _____in the transaction.

5.   The expected close date for the transaction will be based on

        _____

        _____

        _____

        _____

6.   What financial items must be considered when planning the flow of the settlement process?

        _____

        _____

        _____

7.   What are the four most common affinity services that will affect the timeline of the closing?

        _____

        _____

        _____

        _____

        _____

8.   A typical real estate transaction may take between

_____

_____

_____

_____

_____

9.   What items must be completed in order for the closing timeline to be met?

_____

_____

_____

_____

_____

10.   If the delay will be lengthy, create undue hardship for either party, or is objectionable to either party, what might occur?

_____

_____

_____

_____

_____

Chapter 6 – The Sales Contract

1.　The _____ will dictate the _____ and ____ _____ that must be met so the transaction may proceed to closing.

2.　A sales agreement that is correctly prepared and endorsed is a _____ that holds each applicable party _____ for the _____ negotiated within the contract.

3.　The format of the signature should _____ all of the other _____ and _____ _____ included within the package.

4.　When a mortgage lender is involved in the transaction there may be _____ _____ or actions necessary to _____ the closing that do not exist when the transaction is set between private parties.

5.　The description of the property should include

_____

_____

_____

_____

6.　All applicable actions and documents detailed within the sales contract should be completed

_____

_____

_____

_____

7.　Upon receipt of the sales agreement, the escrow agent should note what financial details?

_____

_____

_____

_____

8.   Seller concessions are

_____

_____

_____

_____

_____

9.   If a specific inspection is dictated by the sales agreement, the settlement agent should note

_____

_____

_____

_____

_____

10.   Name five specific terms relating to the title that should be noted

_____

_____

_____

_____

_____

11.   What does a real estate sales contract outline?

_____

_____

_____

_____

_____

12.   List five common alternate names you might encounter for a real estate sales contract.

_____

_____

_____

_____

_____

13. List three alternate names commonly used for the contract for deed.

_____

_____

_____

_____

_____

14. Under a contract for deed, who holds legal title to the property?

_____

_____

_____

_____

15. What does the buyer gain under a contract for deed?

_____

_____

_____

_____

_____

16. Who may assign their interest in the property under a contract for deed?

_____

_____

_____

_____

_____

17. Explain the purpose of an option to purchase

_____

_____

_____

_____

_____

18.   What three possible avenues must you explore when you discover an option to purchase in the chain of title?

_____

_____

_____

_____

_____

Chapter 7 – The Title Search

1. Any matter that becomes a _____ , _____ or other matter against the property must be _____ either prior to close or at closing so that all parties understand what the transfer of the property entails.

2. Title insurance is the guarantee of what the buyer is receiving when they _____ a piece of real property.

3. Title insurance remains in effect until the _____ that is being insured is _____ _____ .

4. Deeds will sometimes contain _____ as to what an individual owner _____ or _____ do with their property.

5. An abstract of title is

    _____

    _____

    _____

    _____

    _____

6. The abstractor will locate specifics of the property such as

    _____

    _____

    _____

    _____

    _____

7. The obtainment of insurance provides the buyer with the assurance

    _____

    _____

    _____

    _____

    _____

8.   Provide three examples of why title insurance could become a critical element in the status of a buyer in the future

_____

_____

_____

_____

_____

9.   If a matter discovered during the title search must be cured, what affect will this have on the closing date?

_____

_____

_____

_____

_____

10.   The title abstractor will search various locations including

_____

_____

_____

_____

_____

Chapter 8 - Deeds

1.   Explain the purpose of the deed

_____

_____

_____

_____

_____

2.   What is considered the best deed a buyer can obtain from a seller?

_____

_____

_____

_____

_____

3.   What does a grant deed warrant?

_____

_____

_____

_____

_____

4.   What does a bargain and sale deed warrant?

_____

_____

_____

_____

5. What is the purpose of a correction deed?

_____

_____

_____

_____

_____

6. The physical transfer of a deed before the death of the grantor is known as

_____

_____

_____

_____

_____

7. List five of the most common covenants you may find in a deed of transfer

_____

_____

_____

_____

_____

8. Explain the purpose of an exception in a deed.

_____

_____

_____

_____

_____

9. The basic bargain and sale deed contains no _____ and only the minimal _____ _____ of a deed.

10. A quitclaim deed provides

_____

_____

_____

_____

_____

Chapter 9 – How Title is Held and Transferred

1.   Concurrent ownership held by _____ or more _____.

2.   The term guardianship refers to the _____ of the property and interest of a _____ _____ or _____ individual.

3.   Any _____ taken by any _____ will affect the title to the property you are closing.

4.   The types of ownership are important for you to understand so that you may:

_____

_____

_____

_____

_____

5.   Name the five unities that may exist.

_____

_____

_____

_____

_____

6.   Name the forms of tenancy.

_____

_____

_____

_____

_____

7.   Name five special entity or individual owners whose interest in real property may require special items of scrutiny.

_____

_____

_____

_____

_____

8.   Sole ownership may be held by

_____

_____

_____

_____

9.   Tenancy by Severalty is also known as sole ownership and means that the ownership of a property is

_____

_____

_____

_____

10.   Concurrent owners share

_____

_____

_____

_____

_____

Chapter 10 – Loan Commitment and Security Instruments

1. A promissory note is a _____ between the _____ and the _____ _____.

2. If a transaction includes seller financing, the _____ is actually the _____

3. The buyer will often be asked to sign a statement _____ their _____ _____.

4. The buyer will often be asked to sign a statement confirming their understanding of the _____ _____ dictated through the mortgage and note documents.

5. A mortgage causes the _____ to be secured against _____ rather than other property or as an unsecured personal loan.

6. While you should gain a familiarity with the closing documents you will witness, you should direct any questions pertaining to the inclusions and specifics

   _____

   _____

   _____

   _____

   _____

7. The inclusions and specifics of the note and mortgage documents should be addressed by the

   _____

   _____

   _____

   _____

   _____

8. What elements must a note contain to be considered binding?

   _____

   _____

   _____

   _____

9.   The buyer will be given a monthly payment breakdown at the closing that details

_____

_____

_____

_____

_____

10.   The mortgage servicing transfer disclosure notice is

_____

_____

_____

_____

_____

Chapter 11 – Verification and Certification

1.   If any questions pertaining to any document should arise during the settlement meeting, you should

_____

_____

_____

_____

_____

2.   If there is no company or individual available to answer any questions that arise, what actions should be taken with regard to specific questions about the transaction or documents?

_____

_____

_____

_____

_____

3.   The itemization of amount financed shows

_____

_____

_____

_____

_____

4.   The Itemization of Amount Financed will include

_____

_____

_____

_____

_____

5. The limited power of attorney granted to the settlement agent of specific mortgage lender provides

_____

_____

_____

_____

_____

6. The limited power of attorney _____ that the signor will receive a copy of all altered documents.

7. The limited power of attorney specifically excludes alterations to the

_____

_____

_____

_____

_____

8. A tax certificate details

_____

_____

_____

_____

_____

9. If property taxes for the subject property being closed are in a delinquency status, the tax certificate will detail

_____

_____

_____

_____

_____

10.   What does it mean to escrow taxes and insurance?

_____

_____

_____

_____

_____

11.   What is the purpose of TIL?

_____

_____

_____

_____

_____

12.   When the credit report plays a role in the funds obtained, a disclosure will be provided explaining

_____

_____

_____

_____

_____

13.   The signature affidavit will be a sampling of

_____

_____

_____

_____

_____

14.   The buyer and lender will _____ the manner in which _____ , _____
        _____ and other recurring outside billings will be handheld.

Chapter 12– Pro-Rata Calculations

1.   What is the purpose of prorating?

_____

_____

_____

_____

_____

2.   Prorations may be based on

_____

_____

_____

_____

_____

3.   Name five items commonly subject to prorating

_____

_____

_____

_____

_____

4.   What is the customary calculation base for the pro-rata calculations?

_____

_____

_____

_____

_____

REAL ESTATE CLOSING - SETTLEMENT AGENT

5.   The four items you must determine before beginning the pro-rata calculations are

_____

_____

_____

_____

_____

6.   If taxes due have not been paid by the seller, the sellers tax portion will be

_____

_____

_____

_____

_____

7.   Special assessments for items such as street improvements and water lines

_____

_____

_____

_____

_____

8.   The entry of each prorated item will be included

_____

_____

_____

_____

_____

Chapter 13 – HUD 1

1. What is a settlement statement?

_____

_____

_____

_____

_____

2. The settlement statement will be considered

_____

_____

_____

_____

_____

3. The seller's portion of the settlement statement

_____

_____

_____

_____

_____

4. Included in the seller's portion of the HUD 1 will be

_____

_____

_____

_____

5. POC items are those that are

_____

_____

_____

_____

6.   POC fees commonly include items such as

_____

_____

_____

_____

_____

7.   All financial matters _____ to the _____ will be included on the settlement statement.

8.   All parties will _____ the settlement statement to confirm that they _____ _____ and _____ with the inclusion.

Chapter 14 – Signing and Post Close

1.   The closing instructions result from

_____

_____

_____

_____

2.   Closing instructions will be generated using pertinent information from the

_____

_____

_____

_____

3.   The closing instructions you will receive are

_____

_____

_____

_____

4.   The closing instructions will specify the

_____

_____

_____

_____

5.   The final entry on most instructions will be

_____

_____

_____

_____

6. What is often the last step that must be taken in order for the lender to release transaction funds?

_____

_____

_____

_____

_____

7. What are the common checks that will be paid from the settlement funds?

_____

_____

_____

_____

_____

8. What is the purpose of the public recordation of the transaction documents?

_____

_____

_____

_____

_____

9. Recording of the transaction documents at the courthouse provides what form of notice to the public?

_____

_____

_____

_____

_____

10. What happens to the certification of recordation?

_____

_____

_____

_____

_____

8.   All parties will _____ the settlement statement to confirm that they _____ _____ and _____ with the inclusion.

Chapter 15 – RESPA

1.   RESPA stands for

_____

_____

_____

_____

_____

2.   Who enforces RESPA?

_____

_____

_____

_____

_____

3.   RESPA deals with

_____

_____

_____

_____

_____

4.   The purposes of RESPA are to:

_____

_____

_____

_____

_____

5.   RESPA prohibits

_____

_____

_____

_____

_____

6.   RESPA restricts

_____

_____

_____

_____

_____

7.   What limitations are placed with regard to property tax and insurance payments?

_____

_____

_____

_____

_____

APPENDIX D

Answer Keys

Introduction
1. Transfer or purchase transaction is completed
2. Closing Escrow   Holding a Settlement Meeting
3. Gift Funds   Seller Concessions   Loan Funding   Any other source available to the borrower
4. Review each document for accuracy and completeness
   Provide the documents to each party for signature
   Provide basic explanations for the documents
   Witness the signing of the documents
5. The division of ongoing expenses or income items between the buyer and the seller
   Primary Lenders with excess deposits

Chapter 1 – Types of Meetings
1. confirm   signatures witness   signatures
2. reviewed   stipulations
3. act   signature   confirmation   transfer
4. representative
5. not   escrow
6. Round Table Meeting   Escrow   1
7. All parties pertinent to the transaction will sit down simultaneously to complete their legal
8. A set of closing instructions specific to their needs in the transaction
9. Every task has been completed or a waiver nullifying the need for a specifically negotiated items has been received from the applicable parties
10. Legal authorization that enables them to act on behalf of a missing party
11. Pertinent to the transaction will sit down simultaneously to complete their legal requirements

Chapter 2 – Party Obligations
1. real estate purchase agreement   guide
2. four
3. The executable deed including any covenants and warranties agreed upon by the parties
   The most recent property tax bill for the property being transferred
   An insurance policy showing current coverage on the property if such a requirement has been negotiated in the sales agreement
   The termite or other inspection as negotiated within the sales agreement
   Deeds or documents showing the removal of any liens or encumbrances discovered during the title search or required by the negotiated sales agreement or lender commitment
   A title commitment and insurance policy
   A survey or survey affidavit
   An offset statement or statement by an owner or lien holder as to the exact balance due on a lien held against the property
   Keys to the property
   If the property is an income producing property, any documents securing or confirming this income
4. Funds available for the purchase price negotiated for the property, settlement costs and any matters that the buyer has agreed to pay before settlement
5. Specific documents for the buyer to sign at the settlement meeting
6. Mortgage   Note   Riders   Addendums
   Any other document they deem necessary to solidify the repayment requirement of the funds provided for the transaction
7. Determine if a valid contract exists, that illustrates the negotiations of the transaction
   Confirm that all parties to the transaction are legally authorized to conduct legal actions through competency, resident status and legal age verification
   Verify that each party is being fairly compensated for the exchange being made through the transaction
   Determine that a legal parcel or property is being transferred between the properties
   Confirm that all parties to the transactions are legally authorized to conduct legal actions through competency, resident status and legal age verification.
8. A statement by an owner or lien holder as to the exact balance due on a lien held against the property
9. That they understand the items they are to bring with them to closing
10. Oversee settlement meeting
    Confirm the identity and legal authority of all parties at the meeting
    Oversee the signing of all documents
    Close escrow
    Record applicable documents
    Pay off all matters

Chapter 3 – Meeting Overviews
1. appointed   act
2. record   legal names
3. neutral   buyer   seller

4. legal form   identification
5. details   documents actions   closing instructions
6. current loan balance   documents loan assumption
7. a closing statement   HUD-1
8. will not be present at the time of the closing
9. these funds will be transferred to the settlement agent and become available for disbursement upon confirmation by the lender that all loan conditions have been satisfied
10. every action that each party must complete before the deed is delivered to the buyer and the purchase funds are delivered to the seller

Chapter 4 – Opening Escrow

1. fees   affinity service providers
2. offset statement   cleared
3. expected close date   sales contract
4. Review the information included in the order and confirm that all of the data that will be needed to proceed is included within the ordering documents
5. date of order
   Property address
   The names and addresses of all owners who hold interest in the property
   The sales price agreed upon for the purchase of the property
   The amount (if any) of the earnest money paid
   The allocation of the earnest money
   The amount, if any, of additional funds placed in escrow or other locations to be credited toward the transaction
6. seller finance   seller concessions   lender funds   any conditions relating to these financial matters
7. name of the real estate agent the commission payment that the real estate agent will receive in the transaction
8. Property Description   Sale inclusions or exclusions   any inspections or reports that must be satisfactorily received
9. the buyer   the seller   the real estate agent   the lender
   another party pertinent to your transaction
10. the exact names of the individuals who will be taking title to the property

Chapter 5 – Potential Delays

1. closing date   sales contract
2. addendum   sales agreement   extends
3. service bills   billings   party
4. last   completion
5. the date the buyer wishes to take possession of the property
   The date the seller wishes to relinquish possession of the property
   The date the seller requires the purchase funds paid for the property
6. the completion of the loan application
   Documentation process to obtain the required purchase money
   The date the seller requires the purchase funds for another purchase
7. the completion of a title search on the subject property
   The issuance of a title insurance policy
   The completion of an appraisal
   The completion of a termite or other inspection report as desired by the buyer, seller, or mortgage lender
8. 15 and 60 days to complete
9. property and owner searches inspections loan stipulations   other matters as negotiated in the sales contract
10. a release will be signed by both the buyer and the seller relieving all parties from their obligations under the contract

Chapter 6 – The Sales Contract

1. sales contract   obligations   agreements
2. binding contract responsible terms
3. match   documents instructions
4. additional requirements   fund
5. physical address city name   county name   deed information
6. on or before the expected closing date set in the transaction
7. the division of transaction expense outlined within the sales contract
   The date set for the pro-rata of fixed expense
   The inclusion or exclusion of mortgage funds and contingency clauses
   The allocation of seller concessions toward closing
   The amount of any earnest money deposits received in relationship to the transaction
8. the specific amount of funds a seller will allocate toward paying a buyer's closing costs out of a sellers closing proceeds
9. information detailing who will pay for the inspection
   When payment for the inspection will be made
   Details pertaining to the actions that will ensue if an inspection is not satisfactory
10. the marketability of the title   the ability to insure the title   restrictions specific to the property
    Easements, rights and privileges   costs pertaining to the search   survey completion and costs
11. all the terms and conditions of the sale between a buyer and a seller
12. offer to purchase option to buy or sell   sales agreement   contract for deed

Contract for purchase
13 land contract   article of agreement   installment land contract
14. the seller
15. possession of the property and equitable title
16. both parties may assign their interest in the property
17. an option to purchase real property is a contract that allows the right to purchase the property to a specific individual at a specific price and within a specific time period
18. establish that the option conveyed has expired in time
Establish that an additional document was created terminating the option

Chapter 7 – The Title Search
1. defect   restriction   addressed
2. purchase
3. interest t   transferred
4. restrictions   may   may not
5. the summary of all recorded documents filed within the public records system that apply to a particular parcel of land
6. the exact description
The estate or interest held by the seller of the property
Any exceptions such as liens, encumbrances, or other defects that exist in relationship to the subject property
Any items or actions take against the property owner that might affect the title to the property
Any other matter that appears in public record with applicability to the transaction may require additional research and become part of the title commitment, exceptions or insurance issuances
7. that if any item was missed during the search process, the buyer will not be responsible for any costs that might arise in the future in relationship to a lack of knowledge
8. a deed could contain a clerical error
Incorrect marital rights might have been entered on a deed of conveyance
Undisclosed heirs in a past property transfer might come forth to claim interest in the property
The signature on a deed transfer documentation by any individual deemed unable to sign such documents like a minor or an incompetent individual
9. additional delays in the closing process may occur while the matter is addressed
10. the county recorders office   the county assessor's office
Other taxing agency records   any pendens indexes
Other public records specific to the property or seller

Chapter 8 - Deeds
1. A deed conveys or transfers ownership interest in land from one person to another
2. general warranty deed
3. the seller who provides a grant-deed warrants only the time that particular owner had possession of the title
4. the bargain and sale deed contains no warranties or covenants.
5. a correction deed is used to correct an error in a previously executed document
6. actual delivery
7. Covenant of seizin   Covenant of enjoyment   Covenant against encumbrances
Covenant of further assurance   Covenant of right to convey   Covenant of Non-Claim
8. an exception is included to withhold or exclude part of the estate or land being conveyed from the transfer
9. covenants   essentials
10. contains no warranties   contains no covenants   does not promise the seller even holds interest in the property

Chapter 9 – How Title is Held and Transferred
1. two   individuals
2. administration minor   incompetent
3. action   interested owner
4. Ensure that you have a full understanding of all potential owners who may have obtained an interest to a piece of real property so that you may ensure that any outstanding interests are removed prior to the close of escrow
5. Unity of Time   Unity of Title   Unity of Possession   Unity of Interest
Unity of Person
6. Tenancy by the Entirety   Joint Tenancy   Tenancy in Common
7. Business Trusts   Credit Unions   Corporations   Aliens
Convicts   Government Entities   Banks or Savings Institutions
8. An Individual   Married Couples   Corporations designed as a single entity
9. Cut off from other individuals and the named individual owns the property alone
10. The Property   Unity   Ownership Interest

Chapter 10 – Loan Commitment and Security Instruments
1. contract   borrower   lender
2. lender   seller
3. confirming   mailing address
4. monthly payment
5. note   real property
6. to the individual or company that generated the documents

7. mortgage lender loan processor   closing team at the lending institution
8. the note must be in writing
   The note must be between a borrower and a lender, both of whom have the ability to enter into a legally binding contract
   The note will state the borrowers promise to pay a certain sum of money and the terms under which those monies will be paid
9. PMI   School Taxes   County Taxes   Insurance Premiums
   Any services required under the mortgage agreement
10. Define any mortgage servicing information known to the mortgage lender at the time of closing and the record of historical transfers of servicing activity by the lender

Chapter 11 – Verification and Certification
1. Direct the question to the company or individual who created the applicable signature requirement
2. the services of a competent attorney should be obtained to gain the needed clarification
3. a legal disclosure document from the lender to the borrower of funds
4. items paid by the lender on the borrower's behalf and then financed as part of the transaction
5. for these specific individuals to correct the typographical or clerical errors on behalf of the signor
6. expressly states
7. interest rate   term, principal balance   principal and interest payments   index or margin of an adjustable rate loan
8. the applicable tax records for the subject property being closed to determine the current payment status
9. the exact payment amount   the date that the tax billing became delinquent
   The taxing authority to which the applicable taxes are owed
10. the buyer will pay a portion of these bills to the lender with each monthly payment
    The lender will then hold the portional payments in an escrow account until the billings become due
    The lender then makes payments for these billings
11. to disclose to the borrower the true cost of the credit that they are obtaining
12. the scores received from the bureaus   the factors contributing to the scores
    The fact that the bureaus do not make a credit determination but rather report the inclusions of the credit profile
13. possible signatures of the buyer
14. negotiate   taxes   insurance

Chapter 12 – Pro-Rata Calculations
1. to allow the buyer and seller to split the cost and income fairly according to the term of ownership
2. the date of closing   another term as negotiated within the sales contract
3. real estate taxes   homeowner's insurance premiums rents received on income producing property
   Other income received from property   expenses incurred on an income producing property
   Oil or other fuel tank filling costs   any utility billing not turned off and paid in full prior to closing
   Any other negotiated matter
4. A 30 day month
5. the number of times taxes are assessed per year   the due date of each tax billing cycle
   the status of the payment of the taxes   the period of time each payment covers
6. deducted from the funds received by the seller at the closing table
7. are typically not prorated
8. in the final settlement statement

Chapter 13– HUD 1
1. HUD 1 that is a statement that itemizes all closing costs payable at the closing or settlement meeting
2. the final authority of all transaction calculations and as such, is a very important document at the closing table
3. breaks down all items on the seller's behalf
4. any liens or mortgages that must be paid to secure a clear title to the property
   Any seller concession toward the buyers closing costs (as negotiated in the sales agreement)
   Any additional charges for which the seller is responsible
   Any prorated items the seller has agreed to pay as negotiated in the sales agreements
   Any other costs the seller has incurred that must be paid at the closing table
5. paid outside of closing before settlement
6. credit reports   appraisals   inspections   other matters that the borrower ordered
7. pertinent   transaction agent
8. sign   understand   agree

Chapter 14 – Signing and Post Close
1. the specifics of all of the tasks and processes that led to the closing
2. sales agreement   addendumscontingencies   title report financing conditions
   Any other matter that occurred during the preparatory phase of the real estate transfer
3. a detailing of the exact steps you must take to finalize the closing
4. various conditions and tasks that must be completed at the actual settlement to legally transfer ownership of the subject property
5. the authorization to disperse funds to the parties owed money in the transaction
6. the providing of the fully endorsed documents to the mortgage lender for review
7. mortgage loans or liens for which the seller is responsible
   The sellers portion of the purchase proceeds
   Any billings that are linked to the transaction such as appraisal fees or inspection costs

Any commission due to the real estate agents

Any other matter that is listed on the instructions or for which an agreed upon bill has been presented during the period leading to the closing

8. to provide security to the buyer, lender, and seller because it makes public all records of the transaction
9. constructive notice
10. this document will become a part of the transaction file and will enable anyone who reviews the file to see who completed the recording functions

Chapter 15 - RESPA

1. Real Estate Settlement Procedures Act
2. HUD
3. closing cost and settlement procedures
4. regulate the processes of closing practices in the United States

   Help consumers in shopping for settlement services

   Eliminate referral fees that increase the costs of certain settlement services
5. specific practices in relationship to the transfer of property that involves a first mortgage loan on a one to four unit dwelling

   A person from giving or accepting any thing of value for referrals of settlement services or businesses

   A person from giving or accepting any part of the charge for services that are not performed
6. the amount of property tax and insurance payments that may be paid in advance at or prior to the closing
7. the amount of property tax and insurance payments that may be paid by a borrower in advance is limited to the owner's share of the taxes and insurance that is due at the time of settlement plus 1/6th of the amount that will become due for these items within a 12-month period